An Invitation to
THE SECRET DOCTRINE

Helena Petrovna Blavatsky
1831 — 1891

An Invitation to
THE SECRET DOCTRINE

H. P. Blavatsky

including

The "Secret Doctrine" and Its Study
by Robert Bowen

The Writing of *The Secret Doctrine*
by Kirby Van Mater

THEOSOPHICAL UNIVERSITY PRESS
PASADENA, CALIFORNIA

THEOSOPHICAL UNIVERSITY PRESS
POST OFFICE BOX C
PASADENA, CALIFORNIA 91109–7107
1994

Text from *The Secret Doctrine* is photographed and reproduced from the original 1888 two-volume edition.

The paper in this book meets the standards for permanence and durability of the Council on Library Resources. ∞

Library of Congress Cataloging-in-Publication Data

Blavatsky, H. P. (Helena Petrovna), 1831–1891. Secret Doctrine. Selections
An invitation to the Secret doctrine / H. P. Blavatsky; including The "Secret doctrine" and its study by Robert Bowen; The writing of the secret doctrine by Kirby Van Mater.
p. cm.
Includes bibliographical references.
ISBN 1-55700-009-3 (alk. paper)
1. Theosophy. I. Blavatsky, H. P. (Helena Petrovna), 1831–1891. Secret doctrine.
BP561.S43 B57 1988
299′.934 20–dc20 89-50118
CIP

Printed at Theosophical University Press
Pasadena, California

Contents

Prefatory Note

SHORTLY AFTER *The Secret Doctrine* was published in November 1888, H. P. Blavatsky met with students in London to answer questions on the Stanzas of Dzyan, those esoteric verses on which the *SD* is an inspired commentary. While notes of meetings held in 1889 had been published in her lifetime as *Transactions of the Blavatsky Lodge*,* apparently notes of later gatherings (1890 until her death in 1891) were not preserved. Providentially, Robert Bowen had recorded his impressions and as much as he could recall of HPB's remarks. His notes lay buried for forty years until his son, Captain P. G. B. Bowen of Dublin, Ireland, on going through his father's papers, discovered them and published extracts in *Theosophy in Ireland* under the heading "The 'Secret Doctrine' and its Study."†

An Invitation to THE SECRET DOCTRINE is a succinct and appealing statement of the *SD*'s principal truths in H. P. Blavatsky's own words. Rather than reading the book page by page she felt it important for the student first to grasp the Three Fundamental Principles on which the whole of the philosophy rests; then to study her Summing Up in volume I, and in volume II her Preliminary Notes which outline three further propositions, and her Conclusion. These selections are here reproduced, and we have added HPB's Preface and the Stanzas of Dzyan, as they set the tone for the entire work. Also included are the last few pages of the *SD*, Commander Bowen's report and, for historical purposes, "The Writing of *The Secret Doctrine*" by Kirby Van Mater, revised from his essay in *Sunrise* (November 1975). A Glossary has been added.

---

*Reissued in 1994 as *Secret Doctrine Commentary: Stanzas I–IV.*

†A reprint appeared in *The Theosophical Forum* (August 15, 1932) and in *Sunrise* (August/September 1985). It forms the basis of Ianthe Hoskins' booklet, *Foundations of Esoteric Philosophy* from the writings of H. P. Blavatsky (1980).

Each of us approaches the *SD* according to our temperament and background: a good many like to roam freely and pursue their own intuitive leads; others like to read it straight through before tracing down specific themes; still others feel overwhelmed by the vast scope of the work and want direction in getting started. Guidelines, however, are two-edged: they can help or they can hinder, encourage or discourage a student. They must be well thought out yet open-ended, for if they are too logically organized they stifle intuition, the faculty we most need for comprehending grand abstract truths.

"Every form, no matter how crude," HPB told her London group, "contains the image of its 'creator' concealed within it. So likewise does an author's work, no matter how obscure, contain the concealed image of the author's knowledge." Bowen was profoundly moved: to think that the *SD* contains knowledge greater even than that of HPB — as it must if "much of it comes from men whose knowledge is immensely wider than hers"; and that anyone, even he, could find in HPB's words "knowledge of which she herself is unconscious." The thought is electric. Now, after a hundred years of the *SD*'s being in circulation, we have a growing sense of its magnitude. Instead of becoming fainter with time, its dynamism is augmented, giving dimension to the mahatmic statement that *The Secret Doctrine* was the "triple production" of her teachers and herself.

To those who are drawn to theosophy and would like to explore the *SD*, *An Invitation* should prove welcome. Longtime students may also find it useful as a refresher course on the genesis and evolutionary destiny of our solar universe and its family of planets and of human and other life-waves of monads that compose and inhabit our earth. To some it will become a faithful companion, by the bedside, on trips, and at those moments when the power and beauty of the Stanzas yield their own blessing.

— Grace F. Knoche

The Theosophical Society
Pasadena, California

August 24, 1988

The "Secret Doctrine" and Its Study*

Being extracts from the notes of personal teachings given by H.P.B. to private pupils during the years 1888 to 1891, included in a large MSS volume left to me by my father, who was one of the pupils.
— P. G. B. Bowen

"H.P.B." was especially interesting upon the matter of "The Secret Doctrine" during the past week. I had better try to sort it all out and get it safely down on paper while it is fresh in my mind. As she said herself it may be useful to someone thirty or forty years hence.

First of all then, "The Secret Doctrine" is only quite a small fragment of the Esoteric Doctrine known to the higher members of the Occult Brotherhoods. It contains, she says, just as much as can be received by the World during this coming century. This raised a question — which she explained in the following way: —

"The World" means Man living in the Personal Nature. This "World" will find in the two volumes of the S.D. all its utmost comprehension can grasp, but no more. But this is not to say that the Disciple who is not living in "The World" cannot find any more in the book than the "World" finds. Every form, no matter how crude, contains the image of its "creator" concealed within it. So likewise does an author's work, no matter how obscure, contain the concealed image of the author's knowledge. From this saying I take it that the S.D. must contain all that H.P.B. knows herself, and a great deal more than that, seeing that much of it comes from men whose knowledge is immensely wider than hers. Furthermore, she implies unmistakably that another may well find knowledge in it which she does not possess herself. It is a stimulating thought to consider that it is possible that I myself may find in H.P.B.'s words knowledge of which she herself is unconscious. She dwelt on this idea a good deal. X said afterwards: "H.P.B. must be losing her grip," meaning, I suppose, confidence in

*Reprinted from *Theosophy in Ireland* (11:1), January-March, 1932.

her own knowledge. But —— and —— and myself also, see her meaning better, I think. She is telling us without a doubt not to anchor ourselves to her as the final authority, nor to anyone else, but to depend altogether upon our own widening perceptions.

(Later note on above: — I was right. I put it to her direct and she nodded and smiled. It is worth something to get her approving smile!) — (Sgd.) Robert Bowen.

At last we have managed to get H.P.B. to put us right on the matter of the study of the S.D. Let me get it down while it is all fresh in mind.

Reading the S.D. page by page as one reads any other book (she says) will only end us in confusion. The first thing to do, even if it takes years, is to get some grasp of the "Three Fundamental Principles" given in the PROEM. Follow that up by study of the RECAPITULATION — the numbered items in the SUMMING UP to Vol. I. (Part I.). Then take the PRELIMINARY NOTES (Vol. II.) and the CONCLUSION (Vol. II.).

H.P.B. seems pretty definite about the importance of the teaching (in the CONCLUSION) relating to the times of coming of the Races and Sub-Races. She put it more plainly than usual that there is really no such thing as a future "coming" of races. "There is neither COMING nor PASSING, but eternal BECOMING," she says. The Fourth Root Race is still alive. So are the Third and Second and First — that is their manifestations on our present plane of substance are present. I know what she means, I think, but it is beyond me to get it down in words. So likewise the Sixth Sub-Race is here, and the Sixth Root Race, and the Seventh, and even people of the coming ROUNDS. After all that's understandable. Disciples and Brothers and Adepts can't be people of the everyday Fifth Sub-Race, for the race is a state of evolution.

But she leaves no question but that, as far as humanity at large goes we are hundreds of years (in time and space) from even the Sixth Sub-Race. I thought H.P.B. showed a peculiar anxiety in her insistence on this point. She hinted at "dangers and delusions" coming through ideas that the New Race had dawned definitely on the World. According to her the duration of a Sub-Race for humanity at large coincides with that of the Sidereal Year (the circle of the earth's axis — about 25,000 years.) That puts the new race a long way off.

We have had a remarkable session on the study of the S.D. during the past three weeks. I must sort out my notes and get the result safely down before I lose them.

She talked a good deal about the "FUNDAMENTAL PRINCIPLE." She says: If one imagines that one is going to get a satisfactory picture of the constitution of the Universe from the S.D. one will get only confusion from its study. It is not meant to give any such final verdict on existence, but to LEAD TOWARDS THE TRUTH. She repeated this latter expression many times.

It is worse than useless going to those whom we imagine to be advanced students (she said) and asking them to give us an "interpretation" of the S.D. They cannot do it. If they try, all they give are cut and dried exoteric renderings which do not remotely resemble the TRUTH. To accept such interpretation means anchoring ourselves to fixed ideas, whereas TRUTH lies beyond any ideas we can formulate or express. Exoteric interpretations are all very well, and she does not condemn them so long as they are taken as pointers for beginners, and are not accepted by them as anything more. Many persons who are in, or who will in the future be in the T.S. are of course potentially incapable of any advance beyond the range of a common exoteric conception. But there are, and will be others, and for them she sets out the following and true way of approach to the S.D.

Come to the S.D. (she says) without any hope of getting the final Truth of existence from it, or with any idea other than seeing how far it may lead TOWARDS the Truth. See in study a means of exercising and developing the mind never touched by other studies. Observe the following rules:

1. No matter what one may study in the S.D. let the mind hold fast, as the basis of its ideation to the following ideas

(a) The FUNDAMENTAL UNITY OF ALL EXISTENCE. This unity is a thing altogether different from the common notion of unity — as when we say that a nation or an army is united; or that this planet is united to that by lines of magnetic force or the like. The teaching is not that. It is that existence is ONE THING, not any collection of things linked together. Fundamentally there is ONE BEING. This BEING has two aspects, positive and negative. The positive is Spirit, or CONSCIOUSNESS. The negative is SUBSTANCE, the subject of consciousness. This Being is the Absolute in its primary manifestation. Being absolute there is nothing outside it. It is ALL-BEING. It is indivisible, else it would not be absolute. If a portion could be separated, that remaining could not be absolute, because there would at once arise the question of COMPARISON between it and the separated part. Comparison is incompatible with any idea of absoluteness. Therefore it is clear that this fundamental ONE EXISTENCE, or Absolute Being must be the REALITY in every form there is.

I said that though this was clear to me I did not think that many in the Lodges would grasp it. "Theosophy," she said, "is for those who can think, or for those who can drive themselves to think, not mental sluggards." H.P.B. has grown very mild of late. "Dumskulls!" used to be her name for the average student.

The Atom, the Man, the God (she says) are each separately, as well as all collectively, Absolute Being in their last analysis, that is their REAL INDIVIDUALITY. It is this idea which must be held always in the background of the mind to form the basis for every conception that arises from study of the S.D. The moment one lets it go (and it is most easy to do so when engaged in any of the many intricate aspects of the Esoteric Philosophy) the idea of SEPARATION supervenes, and the study loses its value.

(b) The second idea to hold fast to is that THERE IS NO DEAD MATTER. Every last atom is alive. It cannot be otherwise since every atom is itself fundamentally Absolute Being. Therefore there is no such thing as "spaces" of Ether, or Akasha, or call it what you like, in which angels and elementals disport themselves like trout in water. That's the common idea. The true idea shows every atom of substance no matter of what plane to be in itself a LIFE.

(c) The third basic idea to be held is that Man is the MICROCOSM. As he is so, then all the Hierarchies of the Heavens exist within him. But in truth there is neither Macrocosm nor Microcosm but ONE EXISTENCE. Great and small are such only as viewed by a limited consciousness.

(d) Fourth and last basic idea to be held is that expressed in the Great Hermetic Axiom. It really sums up and synthesises all the others.

As is the Inner, so is the Outer; as is the Great so is the Small; as it is above, so it is below; there is but ONE LIFE AND LAW; and he that worketh it is ONE. Nothing is Inner, nothing is Outer; nothing is

Great, nothing is Small; nothing is High, nothing is Low, in the Divine Economy.

No matter what one takes as study in the S.D. one must correlate it with those basic ideas.

I suggested that this is a kind of mental exercise which must be excessively fatiguing. H.P.B. smiled and nodded. One must not be a fool (she said) and drive oneself into the madhouse by attempting too much at first. The brain is the instrument of waking consciousness, and every conscious mental picture formed means change and destruction of the atoms of the brain. Ordinary intellectual activity moves on well beaten paths in the brain, and does not compel sudden adjustments and destructions in its substance. But this new kind of mental effort calls for something very different — the carving out of new "brain paths," the ranking in different order of the little brain lives. If forced injudiciously it may do serious physical harm to the brain.

This mode of thinking (she says) is what the Indians call Jnana Yoga. As one progresses in Jnana Yoga one finds conceptions arising which though one is conscious of them, one cannot express nor yet formulate into any sort of mental picture. As time goes on these conceptions will form into mental pictures. This is a time to be on guard and refuse to be deluded with the idea that the new found and wonderful picture must represent reality. It does not. As one works on one finds the once admired picture growing dull and unsatisfying, and finally fading out or being thrown away. This is another danger point, because for the moment one is left in a void without any conception to support one, and one may be tempted to revive the cast-off picture for want of a better to cling to. The true student will, however, work on unconcerned, and presently further formless gleams come, which again in time give rise to a larger and more beautiful picture than the last. But the learner will now know that no picture will ever represent the TRUTH. This last splendid picture will grow dull and fade like the others. And so the process goes on, until at last the mind and its pictures are transcended and the learner enters and dwells in the World of NO FORM, but of which all forms are narrowed reflections.

The True Student of The Secret Doctrine is a Jnana Yogi, and this Path of Yoga is the True Path for the Western student. It is to provide him with sign posts on that Path that the Secret Doctrine has been written.

(Later note: — I have read over this rendering of her teaching to H.P.B. asking if I have got her aright. She called me a silly Dumskull to imagine anything can ever be put in words aright. But she smiled and nodded as well, and said I had really got it better than anyone else ever did, and better than she could do it herself).

I wonder why I am getting all this. It should be passed to the world, but I am too old ever to do it. I feel such a child to H.P.B. yet I am twenty years older than her in actual years.

She has changed much since I met her two years ago. It is marvellous how she holds up in the face of dire illness. If one knew nothing and believed nothing, H.P.B. would convince one that she is something away and beyond body and brain. I feel, especially during these last meetings since she has become so helpless bodily that we are getting teachings from another and higher sphere. We seem to feel and KNOW what she says rather than hear it with our bodily ears. X said much the same thing last night.

(Sgd.), ROBERT BOWEN, Cmdr. R.N.

19th April, 1891.

THE SECRET DOCTRINE:

THE SYNTHESIS

OF

SCIENCE, RELIGION, AND PHILOSOPHY.

BY

H. P. BLAVATSKY,

AUTHOR OF "ISIS UNVEILED."

सत्यात् नास्ति परो धर्मः।

"There is no Religion higher than Truth."

VOL. I.—COSMOGENESIS.

London:

THE THEOSOPHICAL PUBLISHING COMPANY, LIMITED,

7, Duke Street, Adelphi, W.C.

WILLIAM Q. JUDGE,

117, Nassau Street, New York.

THE MANAGER OF THE *THEOSOPHIST*,

Adyar, Madras.

—

1888.

This Work

I Dedicate to all True Theosophists,

In every Country,

And of every Race,

For they called it forth, and for them it was recorded.

PREFACE.

THE Author—the writer, rather—feels it necessary to apologise for the long delay which has occurred in the appearance of this work. It has been occasioned by ill-health and the magnitude of the undertaking. Even the two volumes now issued do not complete the scheme, and these do not treat exhaustively of the subjects dealt with in them. A large quantity of material has already been prepared, dealing with the history of occultism as contained in the lives of the great Adepts of the Aryan Race, and showing the bearing of occult philosophy upon the conduct of life, as it is and as it ought to be. Should the present volumes meet with a favourable reception, no effort will be spared to carry out the scheme of the work in its entirety. The third volume is entirely ready; the fourth almost so.

This scheme, it must be added, was not in contemplation when the preparation of the work was first announced. As originally announced, it was intended that the "Secret Doctrine" should be an amended and enlarged version of "Isis Unveiled." It was, however, soon found that the explanations which could be added to those already put before the world in the last-named and other works dealing with esoteric science, were such as to require a different method of treatment: and consequently the present volumes do not contain, in all, twenty pages extracted from "Isis Unveiled."

The author does not feel it necessary to ask the indulgence of her readers and critics for the many defects of literary style, and the imperfect English which may be found in these pages. She is a foreigner, and her knowledge of the language was acquired late in life. The English tongue is employed because it offers the most widely-diffused medium for conveying the truths which it had become her duty to place before the world.

These truths are in no sense put forward as a *revelation*; nor does the author claim the position of a revealer of mystic lore, now made public for the first time in the world's history. For what is contained in this work is to be found scattered throughout thousands of volumes embodying the scriptures of the great Asiatic and early European religions, hidden under glyph and symbol, and hitherto left unnoticed because of this veil. What is now attempted is to gather the oldest tenets together and to make of them one harmonious and unbroken whole. The sole advantage which the writer has over her predecessors, is that she need not resort to personal speculations and theories. For this work is a partial statement of what she herself has been taught by more advanced students, supplemented, in a few details only, by the results of her own study and observation. The publication of many of the facts herein stated has been rendered necessary by the wild and fanciful speculations in which many Theosophists and students of mysticism have indulged, during the last few years, in their endeavour to, as they imagined, work out a complete system of thought from the few facts previously communicated to them.

It is needless to explain that this book is not the Secret Doctrine in its entirety, but a select number of fragments of its fundamental tenets, special attention being paid to some facts which have been seized upon by various writers, and distorted out of all resemblance to the truth.

But it is perhaps desirable to state unequivocally that the teachings, however fragmentary and incomplete, contained in these volumes, belong neither to the Hindu, the Zoroastrian, the Chaldean, nor the Egyptian religion, neither to Buddhism, Islam, Judaism nor Christianity exclusively. The Secret Doctrine is the essence of all these. Sprung from it in their origins, the various religious schemes are now made to merge back into their original element, out of which every mystery and dogma has grown, developed, and become materialised.

It is more than probable that the book will be regarded by a large section of the public as a romance of the wildest kind; for who has ever even heard ot the book of Dzyan?

The writer, therefore, is fully prepared to take all the responsibility for what is contained in this work, and even to face the charge of having invented the whole of it. That it has many shortcomings she is fully aware; all that she claims for it is that, romantic as it may seem to many, its logical coherence and consistency entitle this new Genesis to rank, at any rate, on a level with the "working hypotheses" so freely accepted by modern science. Further, it claims consideration, not by reason of any appeal to dogmatic authority, but because it closely adheres to Nature, and follows the laws of uniformity and analogy.

The aim of this work may be thus stated: to show that Nature is not "a fortuitous concurrence of atoms," and to assign to man his rightful place in the scheme of the Universe; to rescue from degradation the archaic truths which are the basis of all religions; and to uncover, to some extent, the fundamental unity from which they all spring; finally, to show that the occult side of Nature has never been approached by the Science of modern civilization.

If this is in any degree accomplished, the writer is content. It is written in the service of humanity, and by humanity and the future generations it must be judged. Its author recognises no inferior court of appeal. Abuse she is accustomed to; calumny she is daily acquainted with; at slander she smiles in silent contempt.

De minimis non curat lex.

H. P. B.

London, October, 1888.

Three Fundamental Propositions

The reader has to bear in mind that the Stanzas given treat only of the Cosmogony of our own planetary System and what is visible around it, after a Solar Pralaya. The secret teachings with regard to the Evolution of the Universal Kosmos cannot be given, since they could not be understood by the highest minds in this age, and there seem to be very few Initiates, even among the greatest, who are allowed to speculate upon this subject. Moreover the Teachers say openly that not even the highest Dhyani-Chohans have ever penetrated the mysteries beyond those boundaries that separate the milliards of Solar systems from the "Central Sun," as it is called. Therefore, that which is given, relates only to our visible Kosmos, after a "Night of Brahmâ."

Before the reader proceeds to the consideration of the Stanzas from the Book of Dzyan which form the basis of the present work, it is absolutely necessary that he should be made acquainted with the few fundamental conceptions which underlie and pervade the entire system of thought to which his attention is invited. These basic ideas are few in number, and on their clear apprehension depends the understanding of all that follows; therefore no apology is required for asking the reader to make himself familiar with them first, before entering on the perusal of the work itself.

The Secret Doctrine establishes three fundamental propositions :—

(a) An Omnipresent, Eternal, Boundless, and Immutable PRINCIPLE on which all speculation is impossible, since it transcends the power of human conception and could only be dwarfed by any human expression or similitude. It is beyond the range and reach of thought—in the words of Mandukya, "unthinkable and unspeakable."

To render these ideas clearer to the general reader, let him set out with the postulate that there is one absolute Reality which antecedes all manifested, conditioned, being. This Infinite and Eternal Cause—dimly formulated in the "Unconscious" and "Unknowable" of current European philosophy—is the rootless root of "all that was, is, or ever shall be." It is of course devoid of all attributes and is essentially without any relation to manifested, finite Being. It is "Be-ness" rather than Being (in Sanskrit, *Sat*), and is beyond all thought or speculation.

This "Be-ness" is symbolised in the Secret Doctrine under two aspects. On the one hand, absolute abstract Space, representing bare subjectivity, the one thing which no human mind can either exclude from any conception, or conceive of by itself. On the other, absolute Abstract Motion representing Unconditioned Consciousness. Even our Western thinkers have shown that Consciousness is inconceivable to us apart from change, and motion best symbolises change, its essential characteristic. This latter aspect of the one Reality, is also symbolised by the term "The Great Breath," a symbol sufficiently graphic to need no further elucidation. Thus, then, the first fundamental axiom of the Secret Doctrine is this metaphysical ONE ABSOLUTE—BE-NESS—symbolised by finite intelligence as the theological Trinity.

It may, however, assist the student if a few further explanations are given here.

Herbert Spencer has of late so far modified his Agnosticism, as to assert that the nature of the "First Cause,"* which the Occultist more logically derives from the "Causeless Cause," the "Eternal," and the "Unknowable," may be essentially the same as that of the Consciousness which wells up within us : in short, that the impersonal reality pervading

---

* The "first" presupposes necessarily something which is the "first brought forth," "the first in time, space, and rank"—and therefore finite and conditioned. The "first"

the Kosmos is the pure noumenon of thought. This advance on his part brings him very near to the esoteric and Vedantin tenet.*

Parabrahm (the One Reality, the Absolute) is the field of Absolute Consciousness, *i.e.*, that Essence which is out of all relation to conditioned existence, and of which conscious existence is a conditioned symbol. But once that we pass in thought from this (to us) Absolute Negation, duality supervenes in the contrast of Spirit (or consciousness) and Matter, Subject and Object.

Spirit (or Consciousness) and Matter are, however, tc be regarded, not as independent realities, but as the two facets or aspects of the Absolute (Parabrahm), which constitute the basis of conditioned Being whether subjective or objective.

Considering this metaphysical triad as the Root from which proceeds all manifestation, the great Breath assumes the character of precosmic Ideation. It is the *fons et origo* of force and of all individual consciousness, and supplies the guiding intelligence in the vast scheme of cosmic Evolution. On the other hand, precosmic root-substance (*Mulaprakriti*) is that aspect of the Absolute which underlies all the objective planes of Nature.

Just as pre-Cosmic Ideation is the root of all individual consciousness, so pre-Cosmic Substance is the substratum of matter in the various grades of its differentiation.

Hence it will be apparent that the contrast of these two aspects of the Absolute is essential to the existence of the "Manifested Universe." Apart from Cosmic Substance, Cosmic Ideation could not manifest as individual consciousness, since it is only through a vehicle† of matter that consciousness wells up as "I am I," a physical basis being necessary to focus a ray of the Universal Mind at a certain stage of complexity. Again, apart from Cosmic Ideation, Cosmic Substance would remain an empty abstraction, and no emergence of consciousness could ensue.

The "Manifested Universe," therefore, is pervaded by duality, which is, as it were, the very essence of its EX-istence as "manifestation."

---

cannot be the absolute, for it is a manifestation. Therefore, Eastern Occultism calls the Abstract All the "Causeless One Cause," the "Rootless Root," and limits the "First Cause" to the *Logos*, in the sense that Plato gives to this term.

* See Mr. Subba Row's four able lectures on the Bhagavad Gita, "Theosophist," February, 1887.

† Called in Sanskrit: "Upadhi."

But just as the opposite poles of subject and object, spirit and matter, are but aspects of the One Unity in which they are synthesized, so, in the manifested Universe, there is "that" which links spirit to matter, subject to object.

This something, at present unknown to Western speculation, is called by the occultists Fohat. It is the "bridge" by which the "Ideas" existing in the "Divine Thought" are impressed on Cosmic substance as the "laws of Nature." Fohat is thus the dynamic energy of Cosmic Ideation; or, regarded from the other side, it is the intelligent medium, the guiding power of all manifestation, the "Thought Divine" transmitted and made manifest through the Dhyan Chohans,* the Architects of the visible World. Thus from Spirit, or Cosmic Ideation, comes our consciousness; from Cosmic Substance the several vehicles in which that consciousness is individualised and attains to self—or reflective—consciousness; while Fohat, in its various manifestations, is the mysterious link between Mind and Matter, the animating principle electrifying every atom into life.

The following summary will afford a clearer idea to the reader.

(1.) The ABSOLUTE; the *Parabrahm* of the Vedantins or the one Reality, SAT, which is, as Hegel says, both Absolute Being and Non-Being.

(2.) The first manifestation, the impersonal, and, in philosophy, *unmanifested* Logos, the precursor of the "manifested." This is the "First Cause," the "Unconscious" of European Pantheists.

(3.) Spirit-matter, LIFE; the "Spirit of the Universe," the Purusha and Prakriti, or the *second* Logos.

(4.) Cosmic Ideation, MAHAT or Intelligence, the Universal World-Soul; the Cosmic Noumenon of Matter, the basis of the intelligent operations in and of Nature, also called MAHA-BUDDHI.

The ONE REALITY; its *dual* aspects in the conditioned Universe.

Further, the Secret Doctrine affirms:—

(b.) The Eternity of the Universe *in toto* as a boundless plane; periodically "the playground of numberless Universes incessantly manifesting and disappearing," called "the manifesting stars," and the "sparks of Eternity." "The Eternity of the Pilgrim"† is like a wink

---

* Called by Christian theology: Archangels, Seraphs, etc., etc.

† "Pilgrim" is the appellation given to our *Monad* (the two in one) during its cycle of incarnations. It is the only immortal and eternal principle in us, being an indivisible part of the integral whole—the Universal Spirit, from which it emanates, and into which it is absorbed at the end of the cycle. When it is said to emanate from the one

of the Eye of Self-Existence (Book of Dzyan.) "The appearance and disappearance of Worlds is like a regular tidal ebb of flux and reflux." (See Part II., "Days and Nights of Brahmâ.")

This second assertion of the Secret Doctrine is the absolute universality of that law of periodicity, of flux and reflux, ebb and flow, which physical science has observed and recorded in all departments of nature. An alternation such as that of Day and Night, Life and Death, Sleeping and Waking, is a fact so common, so perfectly universal and without exception, that it is easy to comprehend that in it we see one of the absolutely fundamental laws of the universe.

Moreover, the Secret Doctrine teaches :—

(*c*) The fundamental identity of all Souls with the Universal Over-Soul, the latter being itself an aspect of the Unknown Root ; and the obligatory pilgrimage for every Soul—a spark of the former—through the Cycle of Incarnation (or "Necessity") in accordance with Cyclic and Karmic law, during the whole term. In other words, no purely spiritual Buddhi (divine Soul) can have an independent (conscious) existence before the spark which issued from the pure Essence of the Universal Sixth principle,—or the OVER-SOUL,—has (a) passed through every elemental form of the phenomenal world of that Manvantara, and (b) acquired individuality, first by natural impulse, and then by self-induced and self-devised efforts (checked by its Karma), thus ascending through all the degrees of intelligence, from the lowest to the highest Manas, from mineral and plant, up to the holiest archangel (Dhyani-Buddha). The pivotal doctrine of the Esoteric philosophy admits no privileges or special gifts in man, save those won by his own Ego through personal effort and merit throughout a long series of metempsychoses and reincarnations. This is why the Hindus say that the Universe is Brahma and Brahmâ, for Brahma is in every atom of the universe, the six principles in Nature being all the outcome—the variously differentiated aspects—of the SEVENTH and ONE, the only reality in the Universe whether Cosmical or micro-cosmical ; and also why the permutations (psychic, spiritual and physical), on the plane of manifestation and form, of the sixth (Brahmâ the vehicle of Brahma) are viewed by metaphysical

spirit, an awkward and incorrect expression has to be used, for lack of appropriate words in English. The Vedantins call it Sutratma (Thread-Soul), but their explanation, too, differs somewhat from that of the occultists ; to explain which difference, however, is left to the Vedantins themselves.

antiphrasis as illusive and Mayavic. For although the root of every atom individually and of every form collectively, is that seventh principle or the one Reality, still, in its manifested phenomenal and temporary appearance, it is no better than an evanescent illusion of our senses. (See, for clearer definition, Addendum "Gods, Monads and Atoms," and also "Theophania," "Bodhisatvas and Reincarnation," etc., etc.)

* * *

[p. 20:]

Such are the basic conceptions on which the Secret Doctrine rests.

It would not be in place here to enter upon any defence or proof of their inherent reasonableness; nor can I pause to show how they are, in fact, contained—though too often under a misleading guise—in every system of thought or philosophy worthy of the name.

Once that the reader has gained a clear comprehension of them and realised the light which they throw on every problem of life, they will need no further justification in his eyes, because their truth will be to him as evident as the sun in heaven. I pass on, therefore, to the subject matter of the Stanzas as given in this volume, adding a skeleton outline of them, in the hope of thereby rendering the task of the student more easy, by placing before him in a few words the general conception therein explained.

Stanza I. The history of cosmic evolution, as traced in the Stanzas, is, so to say, the abstract algebraical formula of that Evolution. Hence the student must not expect to find there an account of all the stages and transformations which intervene between the first beginnings of "Universal" evolution and our present state. To give such an account would be as impossible as it would be incomprehensible to men who cannot even grasp the nature of the plane of existence next to that to which, for the moment, their consciousness is limited.

The Stanzas, therefore, give an abstract formula which can be applied, *mutatis mutandis*, to all evolution: to that of our tiny earth, to that of the chain of planets of which that earth forms one, to the solar Universe to which that chain belongs, and so on, in an ascending scale, till the mind reels and is exhausted in the effort.

The seven Stanzas given in this volume represent the seven terms of this abstract formula. They refer to, and describe the seven great stages of the evolutionary process, which are spoken of in the Purânas as the "Seven Creations," and in the Bible as the "Days" of Creation.

The First Stanza describes the state of the ONE ALL during Pralaya, before the first flutter of re-awakening manifestation.

A moment's thought shows that such a state can only be symbolised; to describe it is impossible. Nor can it be symbolised except in negatives; for, since it is the state of Absoluteness *per se*, it can possess none of those specific attributes which serve us to describe objects in positive terms. Hence that state can only be suggested by the negatives of all those most abstract attributes which men feel rather than conceive, as the remotest limits attainable by their power of conception.

The stage described in Stanza II. is, to a western mind, so nearly identical with that mentioned in the first Stanza, that to express the idea of its difference would require a treatise in itself. Hence it must be left to the intuition and the higher faculties of the reader to grasp, as far as he can, the meaning of the allegorical phrases used. Indeed it must be remembered that all these Stanzas appeal to the inner faculties rather than to the ordinary comprehension of the physical brain.

Stanza III. describes the Re-awakening of the Universe to life after Pralaya. It depicts the emergence of the "Monads" from thei state of absorption within the ONE; the earliest and highest stage in the formation of "Worlds," the term Monad being one which may apply equally to the vastest Solar System or the tiniest atom.

Stanza IV. shows the differentiation of the "Germ" of the Universe into the septenary hierarchy of conscious Divine Powers, who are the active manifestations of the One Supreme Energy. They are the framers, shapers, and ultimately the creators of all the manifested Universe, in the only sense in which the name "Creator" is intelligible; they inform and guide it; they are the intelligent Beings who adjust and control evolution, embodying in themselves those manifestations of the ONE LAW, which we know as "The Laws of Nature."

Generically, they are known as the Dhyan Chohans, though each of the various groups has its own designation in the Secret Doctrine.

This stage of evolution is spoken of in Hindu mythology as the "Creation" of the Gods.

In Stanza V. the process of world-formation is described:—First, diffused Cosmic Matter, then the fiery "whirlwind," the first stage in the formation of a nebula. That nebula condenses, and after passing through various transformations, forms a Solar Universe, a planetary chain, or a single planet, as the case may be.

The subsequent stages in the formation of a "World" are indicated in Stanza VI., which brings the evolution of such a world down to its fourth great period, corresponding to the period in which we are now living.

Stanza VII. continues the history, tracing the descent of life down to the appearance of Man; and thus closes the first Book of the Secret Doctrine.

The development of "Man" from his first appearance on this earth in this Round to the state in which we now find him will form the subject of Book II.

PART I.

COSMIC EVOLUTION.

SEVEN STANZAS TRANSLATED WITH COMMENTARIES

FROM THE

SECRET BOOK OF DZYAN.

"Nor Aught nor Nought existed; yon bright sky
Was not, nor heaven's broad roof outstretched above.
What covered all? what sheltered? what concealed?
Was it the water's fathomless abyss?
There was not death—yet there was nought immortal,
There was no confine betwixt day and night;
The only One breathed breathless by itself,
Other than It there nothing since has been.
Darkness there was, and all at first was veiled
In gloom profound—an ocean without light—
The germ that still lay covered in the husk
Burst forth, one nature, from the fervent heat.

. . . .

Who knows the secret? who proclaimed it here?
Whence, whence this manifold creation sprang?
The Gods themselves came later into being—
Who knows from whence this great creation sprang?
That, whence all this great creation came,
Whether Its will created or was mute,
The Most High Seer that is in highest heaven,
He knows it—or perchance even He knows not."

"Gazing into eternity . . .
Ere the foundations of the earth were laid,

. . . . .

Thou wert. And when the subterranean flame
Shall burst its prison and devour the frame . . .
Thou shalt be still as Thou wert before
And knew no change, when time shall be no more.
Oh! endless thought, divine ETERNITY."

COSMIC EVOLUTION.

In Seven Stanzas translated from the Book of Dzyan.

STANZA I.

1. The eternal parent wrapped in her ever invisible robes had slumbered once again for seven eternities.

2. Time was not, for it lay asleep in the infinite bosom of duration.

5. Universal mind was not, for there were no Ah-hi to contain it.

4. The seven ways to bliss were not. The great causes of misery were not, for there was no one to produce and get ensnared by them.

5. Darkness alone filled the boundless all, for father, mother and son were once more one, and the son had not awakened yet for the new wheel, and his pilgrimage thereon.

6. The seven sublime lords and the seven truths had ceased to be, and the Universe, the son of Necessity, was immersed in Paranishpanna, to be outbreathed by that which is and yet is not. Naught was.

7. The causes of existence had been done away with; the visible that was, and the invisible that is, rested in eternal non-being—the one being.

8. Alone the one form of existence stretched boundless, infinite, causeless, in dreamless sleep; and life pulsated unconscious in universal space, throughout that all-presence which is sensed by the opened eye of the Dangma.

9. But where was the Dangma when the Alaya of the universe was in Paramartha and the great wheel was Anupadaka?

STANZA II.

1\. . . . WHERE WERE THE BUILDERS, THE LUMINOUS SONS OF MANVANTARIC DAWN? . . . IN THE UNKNOWN DARKNESS IN THEIR AH-HI PARANISHPANNA. THE PRODUCERS OF FORM FROM NO-FORM—THE ROOT OF THE WORLD—THE DEVAMATRI AND SVÂBHÂVAT, RESTED IN THE BLISS OF NON-BEING.

2\. . . . WHERE WAS SILENCE? WHERE THE EARS TO SENSE IT? NO, THERE WAS NEITHER SILENCE NOR SOUND; NAUGHT SAVE CEASELESS ETERNAL BREATH, WHICH KNOWS ITSELF NOT.

3\. THE HOUR HAD NOT YET STRUCK; THE RAY HAD NOT YET FLASHED INTO THE GERM; THE MATRIPADMA HAD NOT YET SWOLLEN.

4\. HER HEART HAD NOT YET OPENED FOR THE ONE RAY TO ENTER, THENCE TO FALL, AS THREE INTO FOUR, INTO THE LAP OF MAYA.

5\. THE SEVEN SONS WERE NOT YET BORN FROM THE WEB OF LIGHT. DARKNESS ALONE WAS FATHER-MOTHER, SVÂBHÂVAT; AND SVÂBHÂVAT WAS IN DARKNESS.

6\. THESE TWO ARE THE GERM, AND THE GERM IS ONE. THE UNIVERSE WAS STILL CONCEALED IN THE DIVINE THOUGHT AND THE DIVINE BOSOM. . . .

STANZA III.

1\. . . . THE LAST VIBRATION OF THE SEVENTH ETERNITY THRILLS THROUGH INFINITUDE. THE MOTHER SWELLS, EXPANDING FROM WITHIN WITHOUT, LIKE THE BUD OF THE LOTUS.

2\. THE VIBRATION SWEEPS ALONG, TOUCHING WITH ITS SWIFT WING THE WHOLE UNIVERSE AND THE GERM THAT DWELLETH IN DARKNESS: THE DARKNESS THAT BREATHES OVER THE SLUMBERING WATERS OF LIFE. . .

3\. DARKNESS RADIATES LIGHT, AND LIGHT DROPS ONE SOLITARY RAY INTO THE MOTHER-DEEP. THE RAY SHOOTS THROUGH THE VIRGIN EGG THE RAY CAUSES THE ETERNAL EGG TO THRILL, AND DROP THE NON-ETERNAL GERM, WHICH CONDENSES INTO THE WORLD-EGG.

4. THEN THE THREE FALL INTO THE FOUR. THE RADIANT ESSENCE BECOMES SEVEN INSIDE, SEVEN OUTSIDE. THE LUMINOUS EGG, WHICH IN ITSELF IS THREE, CURDLES AND SPREADS IN MILK-WHITE CURDS THROUGHOUT THE DEPTHS OF MOTHER, THE ROOT THAT GROWS IN THE DEPTHS OF THE OCEAN OF LIFE.

5. THE ROOT REMAINS, THE LIGHT REMAINS, THE CURDS REMAIN, AND STILL OEAOHOO IS ONE.

6. THE ROOT OF LIFE WAS IN EVERY DROP OF THE OCEAN OF IMMORTALITY, AND THE OCEAN WAS RADIANT LIGHT, WHICH WAS FIRE, AND HEAT, AND MOTION. DARKNESS VANISHED AND WAS NO MORE; IT DISAPPEARED IN ITS OWN ESSENCE, THE BODY OF FIRE AND WATER, OR FATHER AND MOTHER.

7. BEHOLD, OH LANOO! THE RADIANT CHILD OF THE TWO, THE UNPARALLELED REFULGENT GLORY: BRIGHT SPACE SON OF DARK SPACE, WHICH EMERGES FROM THE DEPTHS OF THE GREAT DARK WATERS. IT IS OEAOHOO THE YOUNGER, THE * * * HE SHINES FORTH AS THE SON; HE IS THE BLAZING DIVINE DRAGON OF WISDOM; THE ONE IS FOUR, AND FOUR TAKES TO ITSELF THREE,† AND THE UNION PRODUCES THE SAPTA, IN WHOM ARE THE SEVEN WHICH BECOME THE TRIDASA (OR THE HOSTS AND THE MULTITUDES). BEHOLD HIM LIFTING THE VEIL AND UNFURLING IT FROM EAST TO WEST. HE SHUTS OUT THE ABOVE, AND LEAVES THE BELOW TO BE SEEN AS THE GREAT ILLUSION. HE MARKS THE PLACES FOR THE SHINING ONES, AND TURNS THE UPPER INTO A SHORELESS SEA OF FIRE, AND THE ONE MANIFESTED INTO THE GREAT WATERS.

8. WHERE WAS THE GERM AND WHERE WAS NOW DARKNESS? WHERE IS THE SPIRIT OF THE FLAME THAT BURNS IN THY LAMP, OH LANOO? THE GERM IS THAT, AND THAT IS LIGHT, THE WHITE BRILLANT SON OF THE DARK HIDDEN FATHER.

9. LIGHT IS COLD FLAME, AND FLAME IS FIRE, AND FIRE PRODUCES HEAT, WHICH YIELDS WATER: THE WATER OF LIFE IN THE GREAT MOTHER.

10. FATHER-MOTHER SPIN A WEB WHOSE UPPER END IS FASTENED TO SPIRIT—THE LIGHT OF THE ONE DARKNESS—AND THE LOWER ONE TO ITS SHADOWY END, MATTER; AND THIS WEB IS THE UNIVERSE SPUN OUT OF THE TWO SUBSTANCES MADE IN ONE, WHICH IS SVÂBHÂVAT.

---

† In the English translation from the Sanskrit the numbers are given in that language, *Eka*, *Chatur*, etc., etc. It was thought best to give them in English.

11. It expands when the breath of fire is upon it; it contracts when the breath of the mother touches it. Then the sons dissociate and scatter, to return into their mother's bosom at the end of the great day, and re-become one with her; when it is cooling it becomes radiant, and the sons expand and contract through their own selves and hearts; they embrace infinitude.

12. Then Svâbhâvat sends Fohat to harden the atoms. Each is a part of the web. Reflecting the "Self-Existent Lord" like a mirror, each becomes in turn a world.

STANZA IV.

1. . . . Listen, ye Sons of the Earth, to your instructors—the Sons of the Fire. Learn, there is neither first nor last, for all is one: number issued from no number.

2. Learn what we who descend from the Primordial Seven, we who are born from the Primordial Flame, have learnt from our fathers. . . .

3. From the effulgency of light—the ray of the ever-darkness—sprung in space the re-awakened energies; the one from the egg, the six, and the five. Then the three, the one, the four, the one, the five—the twice seven the sum total. And these are the essences, the flames, the elements, the builders, the numbers, the arupa, the rupa, and the force of Divine Man—the sum total. And from the Divine Man emanated the forms, the sparks, the sacred animals, and the messengers of the sacred fathers within the holy four.

4. This was the army of the voice—the divine mother of the seven. The sparks of the seven are subject to, and the servants of, the first, the second, the third, the fourth, the fifth, the sixth, and the seventh of the seven. These "sparks" are called spheres, triangles, cubes, lines, and modellers; for thus stands the Eternal Nidana—the Oeaohoo, which is:

5. "DARKNESS" THE BOUNDLESS, OR THE NO-NUMBER, ADI-NIDANA SVÂBHÂVAT :—

I. THE ADI-SANAT, THE NUMBER, FOR HE IS ONE.

II. THE VOICE OF THE LORD SVÂBHÂVAT, THE NUMBERS, FOR HE IS ONE AND NINE.

III. THE "FORMLESS SQUARE."

AND THESE THREE ENCLOSED WITHIN THE ◯ ARE THE SACRED FOUR; AND THE TEN ARE THE ARUPA UNIVERSE. THEN COME THE "SONS," THE SEVEN FIGHTERS, THE ONE, THE EIGHTH LEFT OUT, AND HIS BREATH WHICH IS THE LIGHT-MAKER.

6. THEN THE SECOND SEVEN, WHO ARE THE LIPIKA, PRODUCED BY THE THREE. THE REJECTED SON IS ONE. THE "SON-SUNS" ARE COUNTLESS.

STANZA V.

1. THE PRIMORDIAL SEVEN, THE FIRST SEVEN BREATHS OF THE DRAGON OF WISDOM, PRODUCE IN THEIR TURN FROM THEIR HOLY CIRCUMGYRATING BREATHS THE FIERY WHIRLWIND.

2. THEY MAKE OF HIM THE MESSENGER OF THEIR WILL. THE DZYU BECOMES FOHAT, THE SWIFT SON OF THE DIVINE SONS WHOSE SONS ARE THE LIPIKA, RUNS CIRCULAR ERRANDS. FOHAT IS THE STEED AND THE THOUGHT IS THE RIDER. HE PASSES LIKE LIGHTNING THROUGH THE FIERY CLOUDS; TAKES THREE, AND FIVE, AND SEVEN STRIDES THROUGH THE SEVEN REGIONS ABOVE, AND THE SEVEN BELOW. HE LIFTS HIS VOICE, AND CALLS THE INNUMERABLE SPARKS, AND JOINS THEM.

3. HE IS THEIR GUIDING SPIRIT AND LEADER. WHEN HE COMMENCES WORK, HE SEPARATES THE SPARKS OF THE LOWER KINGDOM THAT FLOAT AND THRILL WITH JOY IN THEIR RADIANT DWELLINGS, AND FORMS THEREWITH THE GERMS OF WHEELS. HE PLACES THEM IN THE SIX DIRECTIONS OF SPACE, AND ONE IN THE MIDDLE—THE CENTRAL WHEEL.

4. FOHAT TRACES SPIRAL LINES TO UNITE THE SIXTH TO THE SEVENTH—THE CROWN; AN ARMY OF THE SONS OF LIGHT STANDS AT EACH ANGLE, AND THE LIPIKA IN THE MIDDLE WHEEL. THEY SAY: THIS IS GOOD, THE

FIRST DIVINE WORLD IS READY, THE FIRST IS NOW THE SECOND. THEN THE "DIVINE ARUPA" REFLECTS ITSELF IN CHHAYA LOKA, THE FIRST GARMENT OF THE ANUPADAKA.

5. FOHAT TAKES FIVE STRIDES AND BUILDS A WINGED WHEEL AT EACH CORNER OF THE SQUARE, FOR THE FOUR HOLY ONES AND THEIR ARMIES.

6. THE LIPIKA CIRCUMSCRIBE THE TRIANGLE, THE FIRST ONE, THE CUBE, THE SECOND ONE, AND THE PENTACLE WITHIN THE EGG. IT IS THE RING CALLED "PASS NOT" FOR THOSE WHO DESCEND AND ASCEND. ALSO FOR THOSE WHO DURING THE KALPA ARE PROGRESSING TOWARDS THE GREAT DAY "BE WITH US." THUS WERE FORMED THE RUPA AND THE ARUPA: FROM ONE LIGHT SEVEN LIGHTS; FROM EACH OF THE SEVEN, SEVEN TIMES SEVEN LIGHTS. THE WHEELS WATCH THE RING. . . . .

STANZA VI.

1. BY THE POWER OF THE MOTHER OF MERCY AND KNOWLEDGE—KWAN-YIN—THE "TRIPLE" OF KWAN-SHAI-YIN, RESIDING IN KWAN-YIN-TIEN, FOHAT, THE BREATH OF THEIR PROGENY, THE SON OF THE SONS, HAVING CALLED FORTH, FROM THE LOWER ABYSS, THE ILLUSIVE FORM OF SIEN-TCHANG AND THE SEVEN ELEMENTS:*

2. THE SWIFT AND RADIANT ONE PRODUCES THE SEVEN LAYA CENTRES, AGAINST WHICH NONE WILL PREVAIL TO THE GREAT DAY "BE-WITH-US," AND SEATS THE UNIVERSE ON THESE ETERNAL FOUNDATIONS SURROUNDING TSIEN-TCHAN WITH THE ELEMENTARY GERMS.

3. OF THE SEVEN—FIRST ONE MANIFESTED, SIX CONCEALED, TWO MANIFESTED, FIVE CONCEALED; THREE MANIFESTED, FOUR CONCEALED; FOUR PRODUCED, THREE HIDDEN; FOUR AND ONE TSAN REVEALED, TWO AND ONE HALF CONCEALED; SIX TO BE MANIFESTED, ONE LAID ASIDE. LASTLY, SEVEN SMALL WHEELS REVOLVING; ONE GIVING BIRTH TO THE OTHER.

* Verse 1 of Stanza VI. is of a far later date than the other Stanzas, though still very ancient. The old text of this verse, having names entirely unknown to the Orientalists would give no clue to the student.

4. He builds them in the likeness of older wheels, placing them on the Imperishable Centres.

How does Fohat build them? he collects the fiery dust. He makes balls of fire, runs through them, and round them, infusing life thereinto, then sets them into motion; some one way, some the other way. They are cold, he makes them hot. They are dry, he makes them moist. They shine, he fans and cools them. Thus acts Fohat from one twilight to the other, during Seven Eternities.

5. At the fourth, the sons are told to create their images. One third refuses—two obey.

The curse is pronounced; they will be born on the fourth, suffer and cause suffering; this is the first war.

6. The older wheels rotated downwards and upwards. . . . The mother's spawn filled the whole. There were battles fought between the Creators and the Destroyers, and battles fought for space; the seed appearing and re-appearing continuously.

7. Make thy calculations, Lanoo, if thou wouldest learn the correct age of thy small wheel. Its fourth spoke is our mother. Reach the fourth "fruit" of the fourth path of knowledge that leads to Nirvana, and thou shalt comprehend, for thou shalt see . . . . .

STANZA VII.

1. Behold the beginning of sentient formless life.

First the Divine, the one from the Mother-Spirit; then the Spiritual; the three from the one, the four from the one, and the five from which the three, the five, and the seven. These are the three-fold, the four-fold downward; the "mind-born" sons of the first Lord; the shining seven.

It is they who are thou, me, him, oh Lanoo. They, who watch over thee, and thy mother earth.

2. THE ONE RAY MULTIPLIES THE SMALLER RAYS. LIFE PRECEDES FORM, AND LIFE SURVIVES THE LAST ATOM OF FORM. THROUGH THE COUNTLESS RAYS PROCEEDS THE LIFE-RAY, THE ONE, LIKE A THREAD THROUGH MANY JEWELS.

3. WHEN THE ONE BECOMES TWO, THE THREEFOLD APPEARS, AND THE THREE ARE ONE ; AND IT IS OUR THREAD, OH LANOO, THE HEART OF THE MAN-PLANT CALLED SAPTASARMA.

4. IT IS THE ROOT THAT NEVER DIES ; THE THREE-TONGUED FLAME OF THE FOUR WICKS. THE WICKS ARE THE SPARKS, THAT DRAW FROM THE THREE-TONGUED FLAME SHOT OUT BY THE SEVEN—THEIR FLAME—THE BEAMS AND SPARKS OF ONE MOON REFLECTED IN THE RUNNING WAVES OF ALL THE RIVERS OF EARTH.

5. THE SPARK HANGS FROM THE FLAME BY THE FINEST THREAD OF FOHAT. IT JOURNEYS THROUGH THE SEVEN WORLDS OF MAYA. IT STOPS IN THE FIRST, AND IS A METAL AND A STONE ; IT PASSES INTO THE SECOND AND BEHOLD—A PLANT ; THE PLANT WHIRLS THROUGH SEVEN CHANGES AND BECOMES A SACRED ANIMAL. FROM THE COMBINED ATTRIBUTES OF THESE, MANU, THE THINKER IS FORMED. WHO FORMS HIM ? THE SEVEN LIVES, AND THE ONE LIFE. WHO COMPLETES HIM ? THE FIVE-FOLD LHA. AND WHO PERFECTS THE LAST BODY ? FISH, SIN, AND SOMA. . . . .

6. FROM THE FIRST-BORN THE THREAD BETWEEN THE SILENT WATCHER AND HIS SHADOW BECOMES MORE STRONG AND RADIANT WITH EVERY CHANGE. THE MORNING SUN-LIGHT HAS CHANGED INTO NOON-DAY GLORY. . . . .

7. THIS IS THY PRESENT WHEEL, SAID THE FLAME TO THE SPARK. THOU ART MYSELF, MY IMAGE, AND MY SHADOW. I HAVE CLOTHED MYSELF IN THEE, AND THOU ART MY VAHAN TO THE DAY, "BE WITH US," WHEN THOU SHALT RE-BECOME MYSELF AND OTHERS, THYSELF AND ME. THEN THE BUILDERS, HAVING DONNED THEIR FIRST CLOTHING, DESCEND ON RADIANT EARTH AND REIGN OVER MEN—WHO ARE THEMSELVES. . . .

Thus ends this portion of the archaic narrative, dark, confused, almost incomprehensible. An attempt will now be made to throw light into this darkness, to make sense out of this apparent NON-SENSE.

SUMMING UP.

"The History of Creation and of this world from its beginning up to the present time is composed of *seven chapters*. The *seventh* chapter is not yet written."
(T. SUBBA ROW, *Theosophist*, 1881.)

THE first of these Seven chapters has been attempted and is now finished. However incomplete and feeble as an exposition, it is, at any rate, an approximation—using the word in a mathematical sense—to that which is the oldest basis for all the subsequent Cosmogonies. The attempt to render in a European tongue the grand panorama of the ever periodically recurring Law—impressed upon the plastic minds of the first races endowed with Consciousness by those who reflected the same from the Universal Mind—is daring, for no human language, save the Sanskrit—which is that *of the Gods*—can do so with any degree of adequacy. But the failures in this work must be forgiven for the sake of the motive.

As a whole, neither the foregoing nor what follows can be found in full anywhere. It is not taught in any of the six Indian schools of philosophy, for it pertains to their synthesis—the seventh, which is the Occult doctrine. It is not traced on any crumbling papyrus of Egypt, nor is it any longer graven on Assyrian tile or granite wall. The Books of the *Vedanta* (the last word of human knowledge) give out but the metaphysical aspect of this world-Cosmogony; and their priceless thesaurus, the *Upanishads*—*Upa-ni-shad* being a compound word meaning "the conquest of ignorance by the revelation of *secret*, *spiritual* knowledge"—require now the additional possession of a Master-key to enable the student to get at their full meaning. The reason for this I venture to state here as I learned it from a Master.

The name, "*Upanishads*," is usually translated "esoteric doctrine." These treatises form part of the *Sruti* or "revealed knowledge," *Revelation*, in short, and are generally attached to the *Brahmana* portion of the Vedas,* as their third division. There are over 150 *Upanishads* enumerated by, and known to, Orientalists, who credit the oldest with being written *probably* about 600 years B.C.; but of *genuine* texts there does not exist a fifth of the number. The Upanishads are to the Vedas what the Kabala is to the Jewish Bible. They treat of and expound the secret and mystic meaning of the Vedic texts. They speak of the origin of the Universe, the nature of Deity, and of Spirit and Soul, as also of the metaphysical connection of mind and matter. In a few words: They CONTAIN *the beginning and the end of all human knowledge, but they have now ceased to* REVEAL *it*, since the day of Buddha. If it were otherwise, the Upanishads could not be called *esoteric*, since they are now openly attached to the Sacred Brahmanical books, which have, in our present age, become accessible even to the *Mlechchhas* (out-*castes*) and the European Orientalists. One thing in them—and this in all the *Upanishads*—invariably and constantly points to their ancient origin, and proves (*a*) that they were written, in some of their portions, *before* the caste system became the tyrannical institution which it still is; and (*b*) that half of their contents have been eliminated, while some of them were rewritten and abridged. "The great Teachers of the higher Knowledge and the Brahmans are continually represented as going to Kshatriya (military caste) kings to become their pupils." As Cowell pertinently remarks, the *Upanishads* "breathe an entirely different spirit" (from other Brahmanical writings), "a freedom of thought unknown in any earlier work except in the Rig Veda hymns themselves." The second fact is explained by a tradition recorded in one of the MSS. on Buddha's life. It says that the Upanishads were originally attached to their Brahmanas after the beginning of a reform, which led to the exclusiveness of the present caste system among the Brahmins, a few centuries after the invasion of India by the "twice-born." They were complete in those days, and were used for the instruction of the chelas who were preparing for their initiation.

* . . . "The Vedas have a distinct dual meaning—one expressed by the literal sense of the words, the other indicated by the metre and the *swara*—intonation—which are as the life of the Vedas. . . . Learned pundits and philologists of course deny that *swara* has anything to do with philosophy or ancient esoteric doctrines; but the mysterious connection between *swara* and *light* is one of its most profound secrets." (T. Subba Row, *Five Years of Theosophy*, p. 154.)

This lasted so long as the Vedas and the Brahmanas remained in the sole and exclusive keeping of the temple-Brahmins—while no one else had the right to study or even read them outside of the *sacred* caste. Then came Gautama, the Prince of Kapilavastu. After *learning* the whole of the Brahmanical wisdom in the *Rahasya* or the *Upanishads*, and finding that the teachings differed little, if at all, from those of the "Teachers of Life" inhabiting the snowy ranges of the Himalaya, * the Disciple of the Brahmins, feeling indignant because the sacred wisdom was thus withheld from all but the Brahmins, determined to save the whole world by popularizing it. Then it was that the Brahmins, seeing that their sacred knowledge and Occult wisdom was falling into the hands of the "*Mlechchhas*," abridged the texts of the Upanishads, originally containing thrice the matter of the Vedas and the Brahmanas together, without altering, however, one word of the texts. They simply detached from the MSS. the most important portions containing the last word of the Mystery of Being. The key to the Brahmanical secret code remained henceforth with the initiates alone, and the Brahmins were thus in a position to publicly deny the correctness of Buddha's teaching by appealing to their *Upanishads*, silenced for ever on the chief questions. Such is the esoteric tradition beyond the Himalayas.

Sri Sankaracharya, the greatest Initiate living in the historical ages, wrote many a Bhâshya on the *Upanishads*. But his original treatises, as there are reasons to suppose, have not yet fallen into the hands of the Philistines, for they are too jealously preserved in his *maths* (monasteries, *mathams*). And there are still weightier reasons to believe that the priceless Bhâshyas (Commentaries) on the esoteric doctrine of the Brahmins, by their greatest expounder, will remain for ages yet a dead letter to most of the Hindus, except the *Smârtava* Brahmins. This sect, founded by Sankaracharya, (which is still very powerful in Southern India) is now almost the only one to produce students who have preserved sufficient knowledge to comprehend the

* Also called "the Sons of Wisdom," and of the "Fire-Mist" and the "Brothers of the Sun" in the Chinese records. *Si-dzang* (Tibet) is mentioned in the MSS. of the sacred library of the province of Fo-Kien, as the great seat of Occult learning from time immemorial, ages before Buddha. The Emperor Yu, the "great" (2,207 years B.C.), a pious mystic and great adept, is said to have obtained his knowledge from the "great teachers of the Snowy Range" in Si-dzang.

dead letter of the Bhashyas. The reason of this is that they alone, I am informed, have occasionally real Initiates at their head in their mathams, as for instance, in the "Sringa-giri," in the Western Ghauts of Mysore. On the other hand, there is no sect in that desperately exclusive caste of the Brahmins, more exclusive than is the Smârtava; and the reticence of its followers to say what they may know of the Occult sciences and the esoteric doctrine, is only equalled by their pride and learning.

Therefore the writer of the present statement must be prepared beforehand to meet with great opposition and even the denial of such statements as are brought forward in this work. Not that any claim to infallibility, or to perfect correctness in every detail of all that which is herein said, was ever put forward. Facts are there, and they can hardly be denied. But, owing to the intrinsic difficulties of the subjects treated, and the almost insurmountable limitations of the English tongue (as of all other European languages) to express certain ideas, it is more than probable that the writer has failed to present the explanations in the best and in the clearest form; yet all that could be done was done under every adverse circumstance, and this is the utmost that can be expected of any writer.

Let us recapitulate and show, by the vastness of the subjects expounded, how difficult, if not impossible, it is to do them full justice.

(1.) The Secret Doctrine is the accumulated Wisdom of the Ages, and its cosmogony alone is the most stupendous and elaborate system: *e.g.*, even in the exotericism of the Purânas. But such is the mysterious power of Occult symbolism, that the facts which have actually occupied countless generations of initiated seers and prophets to marshal, to set down and explain, in the bewildering series of evolutionary progress, are all recorded on a few pages of geometrical signs and glyphs. The flashing gaze of those seers has penetrated into the very kernel of matter, and recorded the soul of things there, where an ordinary profane, however learned, would have perceived but the external work of form. But modern science believes not in the "soul of things," and hence will reject the whole system of ancient cosmogony. It is useless to say that the system in question is no fancy of one or several isolated individuals. That it is the uninterrupted record covering thousands of generations of Seers whose respective experiences were made to test and to verify the traditions passed orally by one early race to another, of the teachings of higher and exalted beings, who watched over the childhood of Humanity. That for long ages, the "Wise Men" of the Fifth Race, of the stock saved and rescued from the last cataclysm and shifting of continents, had passed their lives *in learning, not teaching*. How did they do so? It is answered: by checking, testing, and verifying in every department of nature the traditions of old by the independent visions of great adepts; *i.e.*, men who have developed and perfected their physical, mental, psychic, and spiritual organisations to the utmost possible degree. No vision of one adept was accepted till it was checked and confirmed by the visions—so obtained as to stand as independent evidence—of other adepts, and by centuries of experiences.

(2.) The fundamental Law in that system, the central point from which all emerged, around and toward which all gravitates, and upon which is hung the philosophy of the rest, is the One homogeneous divine SUBSTANCE-PRINCIPLE, the one radical cause.

> . . . "Some few, whose lamps shone brighter, have been led
> From cause to cause to nature's secret head,
> And found that one first Principle must be. . . ."

It is called "Substance-Principle," for it becomes "substance" on the plane of the manifested Universe, an illusion, while it remains a "principle" in the beginningless and endless abstract, visible and invisible SPACE. It is the omnipresent Reality: impersonal, because it contains all and everything. *Its impersonality is the fundamental conception* of the System. It is latent in every atom in the Universe, and is the Universe itself. (See in chapters on Symbolism, "Primordial Substance, and Divine Thought.")

(3.) The Universe is the periodical manifestation of this unknown Absolute Essence. To call it "essence," however, is to sin against the very spirit of the philosophy. For though the noun may be derived in this case from the verb *esse*, "to be," yet IT cannot be identified with a *being* of any kind, that can be conceived by human intellect. IT is best described as neither Spirit nor matter, but both. "Parabrahmam and Mûlaprakriti" are One, in reality, yet two in the Universal conception of the manifested, even in the conception of the One Logos, its first manifestation, to which, as the able lecturer in the "Notes on the Bhagavadgita" shows, IT appears from the objective standpoint of the One Logos as Mulaprakriti and not as Parabrahmam; as its *veil* and not the one REALITY hidden behind, which is unconditioned and absolute.

(4.) The Universe is called, with everything in it, MAYA, because all is temporary therein, from the ephemeral life of a fire-fly to that of the Sun. Compared to the eternal immutability of the ONE, and the changelessness of that Principle, the Universe, with its evanescent ever-changing forms, must be necessarily, in the mind of a philosopher, no better than a will-o'-the-wisp. Yet, the Universe is real enough to the conscious beings in it, which are as unreal as it is itself.

(5.) Everything in the Universe, throughout all its kingdoms, is CONSCIOUS: *i.e.*, endowed with a consciousness of its own kind and on its own plane of perception. We men must remember that because *we* do not perceive any signs—which we can recognise—of consciousness, say, in stones, we have no right to say that *no consciousness exists there*. There is no such thing as either "dead" or "blind" matter, as there is no "Blind" or "Unconscious" Law. These find no place among the conceptions of Occult philosophy. The latter never stops at surface appearances, and for it the *noumenal* essences have more reality than their objective counterparts; it resembles therein the mediæval *Nominalists*, for whom it was the Universals that were the realities and the particulars which existed only in name and human fancy.

(6.) The Universe is worked and *guided* from *within outwards*. As above so it is below, as in heaven so on earth; and man—the microcosm and miniature copy of the macrocosm—is the living witness to this Universal Law and to the mode of its action. We see that every *external* motion, act, gesture, whether voluntary or mechanical, organic or mental, is produced and preceded by *internal* feeling or emotion, will or volition, and thought or mind. As no outward motion or change, when normal, in man's external body can take place unless provoked by an inward impulse, given through one of the three functions named, so with the external or manifested Universe. The whole Kosmos is guided, controlled, and animated by almost endless series of Hierarchies of sentient Beings, each having a mission to perform, and who—whether we give to them one name or another, and call them Dhyan-Chohans or Angels—are "messengers" in the sense only that they are the agents of Karmic and Cosmic Laws. They vary infinitely in their respective degrees of consciousness and intelligence ; and to call them all pure Spirits without any of the earthly alloy "which time is wont to prey upon" is only to indulge in poetical fancy. For each of these Beings either *was*, or prepares to become, a man, if not in the present, then in a past or a coming cycle (Manvantara). They are *perfected*, when not *incipient*, men ; and differ morally from the terrestrial human beings on their higher (less material) spheres, only in that they are devoid of the feeling of personality and of the *human* emotional nature—two purely earthly characteristics. The former, or the "perfected," have become free from those feelings, because (*a*) they have no longer fleshly bodies—an ever-numbing weight on the Soul; and (*b*) the pure spiritual element being left untrammelled and more free, they are less influenced by *maya* than man can ever be, unless he is an adept who keeps his two personalities—the spiritual and the physical—entirely separated. The incipient monads, having never had terrestrial bodies yet, can have no sense of personality or EGO-ism. That which is meant by "personality," being a limitation and a relation, or, as defined by Coleridge, "individuality existing in itself but with a nature as a ground," the term cannot of course be applied to non-human entities; but, as a fact insisted upon by generations of Seers, none of these Beings, high or low, have either individuality or personality as separate Entities, *i.e.*, they have no individuality in the sense in which a man says, "*I am myself* and no one else ;" in other words, they are conscious of no such distinct separateness as men and things have on earth. Individuality is the characteristic of their respective hierarchies, not of their units ; and these characteristics vary only with the degree of the plane to which those hierarchies belong : the nearer to the region of Homogeneity and the One Divine, the purer and the less accentuated that individuality in the Hierarchy. They are finite, in all respects, with the exception of their higher principles—the immortal sparks reflecting the universal divine flame—individualized and separated only on the spheres of Illusion by a differentiation as illusive as the rest. They are "Living Ones," because they are the streams projected on the Kosmic screen of illusion from the ABSOLUTE LIFE ; beings in whom life cannot become extinct, before the fire of ignorance is extinct in those who sense these "Lives." Having sprung into being under the quickening influence of the uncreated beam, the reflection of the great Central Sun that radiates on the shores of the river of Life, it is the inner principle in them which belongs to the waters of immortality, while its differentiated clothing is as perishable as man's body. Therefore Young was right in saying that

"Angels are men of a superior kind"

and no more. They are neither "ministering" nor "protecting" angels; nor are they "Harbingers of the Most High" still less the "Messengers of wrath" of any God such as man's fancy has created. To appeal to their protection is as foolish as to believe that their sympathy may be secured by any kind of propitiation; for they are, as much as man himself is, the slaves and creatures of immutable Karmic and Kosmic law. The reason for it is evident. Having no elements of personality in their essence they can have no personal qualities, such as attributed by men, in their exoteric religions, to their anthropomorphic God—a jealous and exclusive God who rejoices and feels wrathful, is pleased with sacrifice, and is more despotic in his vanity than any finite foolish man. Man, as shown in Book II., being a compound of the essences of all those celestial Hierarchies may succeed in making himself, as such, superior, in one sense, to any hierarchy or class, or even combination of them. "Man can neither propitiate nor command the *Devas*," it is said. But, by paralyzing his lower personality, and arriving thereby at the full knowledge of the *non-separateness* of his higher SELF from the One absolute SELF, man can, even during his terrestrial life, become as "One of Us." Thus it is, by eating of the fruit of knowledge which dispels ignorance, that man becomes like one of the Elohim or the Dhyanis; and once on *their* plane the Spirit of Solidarity and perfect Harmony, which reigns in every Hierarchy, must extend over him and protect him in every particular.

The chief difficulty which prevents men of science from believing in divine as well as in nature Spirits is their materialism. The main impediment before the Spiritualist which hinders him from believing in the same, while preserving a blind belief in the "Spirits" of the Departed, is the general ignorance of all, except some Occultists and Kabalists, about the true essence and nature of matter. It is on the acceptance or rejection of the theory of the *Unity of all in Nature, in its ultimate Essence*, that mainly rests the belief or unbelief in the existence around us of other conscious beings besides the Spirits of the Dead.

It is on the right comprehension of the primeval Evolution of Spirit-Matter and its real essence that the student has to depend for the further elucidation in his mind of the Occult Cosmogony, and for the only sure clue which can guide his subsequent studies.

In sober truth, as just shown, every "Spirit" so-called is either a *disembodied or a future man.* As from the highest Archangel (Dhyan Chohan) down to the last conscious "Builder" (the inferior class of Spiritual Entities), all such are *men*, having lived æons ago, in other Manvantaras, on this or other Spheres; so the inferior, semi-intelligent and non-intelligent Elementals—are all *future* men. That fact alone—that a Spirit is endowed with intelligence—is a proof to the Occultist that that Being must have been a *man*, and acquired his knowledge and intelligence throughout the human cycle. There is but one indivisible and absolute Omniscience and Intelligence in the Universe, and this thrills throughout every atom and infinitesimal point of the whole finite Kosmos which hath no bounds, and which people call SPACE, considered independently of anything contained in it. But the first differentiation of its *reflection* in the manifested World is purely Spiritual, and the Beings generated in it are not endowed with a consciousness that has any relation to the one we conceive of. They can have no human consciousness or Intelligence before they have acquired such, personally and individually. This may be a mystery, yet it is a fact, in Esoteric philosophy, and a very apparent one too.

The whole order of nature evinces a progressive march towards *a higher life.* There is design in the action of the seemingly blindest forces. The whole process of evolution with its endless adaptations is a proof of this. The immutable laws that weed out the weak and feeble species, to make room for the strong, and which ensure the "survival of the fittest," though so cruel in their immediate action—all are working toward the grand end. The very *fact* that adaptations *do* occur, that the fittest *do* survive in the struggle for existence, shows that what is called "unconscious Nature"* is in reality an aggregate of forces mani-

---

* Nature taken in its abstract sense, *cannot* be "unconscious," as it is the emanation from, and thus an aspect (on the manifested plane) of the ABSOLUTE consciousness. Where is that daring man who would presume to deny to vegetation and even to minerals *a consciousness of their own.* All he can say is, that this consciousness is beyond his comprehension.

pulated by semi-intelligent beings (Elementals) guided by High Planetary Spirits, (Dhyan Chohans), whose collective aggregate forms the manifested *verbum* of the unmanifested LOGOS, and constitutes at one and the same time the MIND of the Universe and its immutable LAW.

Three distinct representations of the Universe in its three distinct aspects are impressed upon our thought by the esoteric philosophy: the PRE-EXISTING (evolved from) the EVER-EXISTING; and the PHENOMENAL—the world of illusion, the reflection, and shadow thereof. During the great mystery and drama of life known as the Manvantara, real Kosmos is like the object placed behind the white screen upon which are thrown the Chinese shadows, called forth by the magic lantern. The actual figures and things remain invisible, while the wires of evolution are pulled by the unseen hands; and men and things are thus but the reflections, *on* the white field, of the realities *behind* the snares of *Mahamaya*, or the great Illusion. This was taught in every philosophy, in every religion, *ante* as well as *post* diluvian, in India and Chaldea, by the Chinese as by the Grecian Sages. In the former countries these three Universes were allegorized, in exoteric teachings, by the three trinities emanating from the Central eternal germ and forming with it a Supreme Unity: the *initial*, the *manifested*, and the *Creative* Triad, or the three in One. The last is but the symbol, in its concrete expression, of the first *ideal* two. Hence Esoteric philosophy passes over the necessarianism of this purely metaphysical conception, and calls the first one, only, the Ever Existing. This is the view of every one of the six great schools of Indian philosophy—the *six principles of that unit body of* WISDOM *of which the* "*gnosis*," the *hidden* knowledge, is the seventh.

The writer hopes that, superficially handled as may be the comments on the Seven Stanzas, enough has been given in this cosmogonic portion of the work to show Archaic teachings to be more *scientific* (in the modern sense of the word) on their very face, than any other ancient Scriptures left to be regarded and judged on their exoteric aspect. Since, however, as confessed before, this work *withholds far more than it gives out*, the student is invited to use his own intuitions. Our chief care is to elucidate that which has already been given out, and, to our regret, very incorrectly at times; to supplement the knowledge hinted at—whenever and wherever possible—by additional matter; and to bulwark our doctrines against the too strong attacks of modern Sectarianism, and more especially against those of our latter-day Materialism, very often miscalled Science, whereas, in reality, the words "Scientists" and "Sciolists" ought alone to bear the responsibility for the many illogical theories offered to the world. In its great ignorance, the public, while blindly accepting everything that emanates from "authorities," and feeling it to be its duty to regard every *dictum* coming from a man of Science as a proven fact—the public, we say, is taught to scoff at anything brought forward from "heathen" sources. Therefore, as materialistic Scientists can be fought solely with their own weapons—those of controversy and argument—an *Addendum* is added to every Book contrasting our respective views and showing how even great authorities may often err. We believe that this can be done effectually by showing the weak points of our opponents, and by proving their too frequent sophisms—made to pass for scientific *dicta*—to be incorrect. We hold to Hermes and his "Wisdom"—in its universal character; they—to Aristotle as against intuition and the experience of the ages, fancying that Truth is the exclusive property of the Western world. Hence the disagreement. As Hermes says, "Knowledge differs much from sense; for sense is of things that surmount it, but Knowledge (*gyi*) is the end of sense"—*i.e.*, of the illusion of our physical brain and its intellect; thus emphasizing the contrast between the laboriously acquired knowledge of the senses and mind (manas), and the intuitive omniscience of the Spiritual divine Soul—Buddhi.

Whatever may be the destiny of these actual writings in a remote future, we hope to have proven so far the following facts:

(1) The Secret Doctrine teaches no *Atheism*, except in the Hindu sense of the word *nastika*, or the rejection of *idols*, including every anthropomorphic god. In this sense every Occultist is a *Nastika*.

(2) It admits a Logos or a collective "Creator" of the Universe; a *Demi-urgos*—in the sense implied when one speaks of an "Architect" as the "Creator" of an edifice, whereas that Architect has never touched one stone of it, but, while furnishing the plan, left all the manual labour to the masons; in our case the plan was furnished by the Ideation of the Universe, and the constructive labour was left to the Hosts of intelligent Powers and Forces. But that *Demiurgos* is no

personal deity,—*i.e.*, an imperfect *extra-cosmic god*,—but only the aggregate of the Dhyan-Chohans and the other forces.

As to the latter—

(3) They are dual in their character; being composed of (*a*) the irrational *brute energy*, inherent in matter, and (*b*) the intelligent soul or cosmic consciousness which directs and guides that energy, and which is the *Dhyan-Chohanic thought reflecting the Ideation of the Universal mind.* This results in a perpetual series of physical manifestations and *moral effects* on Earth, during manvantaric periods, the whole being subservient to Karma. As that process is not always perfect; and since, however many proofs it may exhibit of a guiding intelligence behind the veil, it still shows gaps and flaws, and even results very often in evident failures—therefore, neither the collective Host (Demiurgos), nor any of the working powers individually, are proper subjects for divine honours or worship. All are entitled to the grateful reverence of Humanity, however, and man ought to be ever striving to help the divine evolution of *Ideas*, by becoming to the best of his ability a *co-worker with nature* in the cyclic task. The ever unknowable and incognizable *Karana* alone, the *Causeless* Cause of all causes, should have its shrine and altar on the holy and ever untrodden ground of our heart—invisible, intangible, unmentioned, save through "the still small voice" of our spiritual consciousness. Those who worship before it, ought to do so in the silence and the sanctified solitude of their Souls *; making their spirit the sole mediator between them and the *Universal Spirit*, their good actions the only priests, and their sinful intentions the only visible and objective sacrificial victims to the *Presence*. *(See Part II., "On the Hidden Deity.")*

(4) Matter is *Eternal*. It is the *Upadhi* (the physical basis) for the One infinite Universal Mind to build thereon its ideations. Therefore, the Esotericists maintain that there is no inorganic or *dead* matter in nature, the distinction between the two made by Science being as unfounded as it is arbitrary and devoid of reason.

* "When thou prayest, thou shalt not be as the hypocrites are . . . but enter into *thine inner chamber and having shut thy door, pray to thy Father which is in secret.*" *Matt. vi.*). Our Father is *within us* "in Secret," our 7th principle, in the "inner chamber" of our Soul perception. "The Kingdom of Heaven" and of God "*is within us*" says Jesus, not *outside*. Why are Christians so absolutely blind to the self-evident meaning of the words of wisdom they delight in mechanically repeating?

Whatever Science may think, however—and *exact* Science is a fickle dame, as we all know by experience—Occultism knows and teaches differently, from time immemorial—from *Manu* and *Hermes* down to Paracelsus and his successors.

Thus, Hermes, the thrice great Trismegistus, says: "Oh, my son, matter *becomes;* formerly it *was;* for matter is the vehicle of becoming.* Becoming is the mode of activity of the uncreate deity. Having been endowed with the germs of becoming, matter (objective) is brought into birth, for the creative force fashions it *according to the ideal forms.* Matter not yet engendered had no form; it becomes when it is put into operation." (*The Definitions of Asclepios*, p. 134, "Virgin of the World.")

"Everything is the product of one universal creative effort. . . . There is nothing *dead* in Nature. *Everything is organic and living*, and therefore the whole world appears to be a living organism." (Paracelsus, "*Philosophia ad Athenienses*," F. Hartmann's translations, p. 44.)

(5.) The Universe was evolved out of its ideal plan, upheld through Eternity in the unconsciousness of that which the Vedantins call Parabrahm. This is practically identical with the conclusions of the highest Western Philosophy—"the innate, eternal, and self-existing Ideas" of Plato, now reflected by Von Hartmann. The "unknowable" of Herbert Spencer bears only a faint resemblance to that transcendental *Reality* believed in by Occultists, often appearing merely a personification of a "*force* behind phenomena"—an infinite and eternal *Energy*

* To this the late Mrs. (Dr.) Kingsford, the able translater and compiler of the Hermetic Fragments (see "*The Virgin of the World*") remarks in a foot-note; "Dr. Menard observes that in Greek the same word signifies *to be born* and *to become*. The idea here is that the material of the world is in its essence eternal, but that before creation or 'becoming' it is in a passive and motionless condition. Thus it 'was' before being put into operation; now it 'becomes,' that is, it is mobile and progressive." And she adds the purely Vedantic doctrine of the Hermetic philosophy that "Creation is thus the period of activity (Manvantara) of God, who, according to Hermetic thought (or *which*, according to the Vedantin) has two modes—Activity or Existence, God evolved (*Deus explicitus*); and Passivity of Being (Pralaya) God involved (*Deus implicitus*). Both modes are perfect and complete, as are the waking and sleeping states of man. Fichte, the German philosopher, distinguished Being (Seyn) as One, which we know only through existence (Daseyn) as the Manifold. This view is thoroughly Hermetic. The 'Ideal Forms' are the archetypal or formative ideas of the Neo-Platonists; the eternal and subjective concepts of things subsisting in the divine mind prior to 'becoming'" (p. 134).

from which all things proceed, while the author of the "Philosophy of the Unconscious" has come (in this respect only) as near to a solution of the great *Mystery* as mortal man can. Few were those, whether in ancient or mediæval philosophy, who have dared to approach the subject or even hint at it. Paracelsus mentions it inferentially. His ideas are admirably synthesized by Dr. F. Hartmann, F.T.S., in his "Life of Paracelsus."

All the *Christian* Kabalists understood well the Eastern root idea: The active Power, the "Perpetual motion of the great Breath" only awakens Kosmos at the dawn of every new Period, setting it into motion by means of the two contrary Forces,* and thus causing it to become objective on the plane of Illusion. In other words, that dual motion transfers Kosmos from the plane of the Eternal Ideal into that of finite manifestation, or from the *Noumenal* to the *phenomenal* plane. Everything that *is*, *was*, and *will be*, eternally IS, even the countless forms, which are finite and perishable only in their objective, not in their *ideal* Form. They existed as Ideas, in the Eternity,† and, when they pass away, will exist as reflections. Neither the form of man, nor that of any animal, plant or stone has ever been *created*, and it is only on this plane of ours that it commenced "becoming," *i.e.*, objectivising into its present materiality, or expanding *from within outwards*, from the most sublimated and supersensuous essence into its grossest appearance. Therefore *our* human forms have existed in the Eternity as astral or ethereal prototypes; according to which models, the Spiritual Beings (or Gods) whose duty it was to bring them into objective being and terrestrial Life, evolved the protoplasmic forms of the future *Egos* from *their own essence*. After which, when this human *Upadhi*, or basic mould was ready, the natural terrestrial Forces began to work on those supersensuous moulds *which contained, besides their own, the elements of all the past vegetable and future animal forms of this globe in them.* Therefore, man's *outward* shell passed through every vegetable and animal body before it assumed the human shape.

* The centripetal and the centrifugal forces, which are male and female, positive and negative, physical and spiritual, the two being the one *Primordial* Force.

† Occultism teaches that no form can be given to anything, either by nature or by man, whose ideal type does not already exist on the subjective plane. More than this; that no such form or shape can possibly enter man's consciousness, or evolve in his imagination, which does not exist in prototype, at least as an approximation.

THE SECRET DOCTRINE:

THE SYNTHESIS
OF
SCIENCE, RELIGION, AND PHILOSOPHY.

BY

H. P. BLAVATSKY,

AUTHOR OF "ISIS UNVEILED."

सत्यात् नास्ति परो धर्मः ।

"There is no Religion higher than Truth."

Vol. II.—ANTHROPOGENESIS.

London:
THE THEOSOPHICAL PUBLISHING COMPANY, LIMITED.
7, Duke Street, Adelphi, W.C.
WILLIAM Q. JUDGE,
117, Nassau Street, New York.
THE MANAGER OF THE *THEOSOPHIST*,
Adyar, Madras.

1888.

MODERN science insists upon the doctrine of evolution; so do human reason and the "Secret Doctrine," and the idea is corroborated by the ancient legends and myths, and even by the Bible itself when it is read between the lines. We see a flower slowly developing from a bud, and the bud from its seed. But whence the latter, with all its predetermined programme of physical transformation, and its invisible, therefore *spiritual* forces which gradually develop its form, colour, and odour? The word *evolution* speaks for itself. The germ of the present human race must have preëxisted in the parent of this race, as the seed, in which lies hidden the flower of next summer, was developed in the capsule of its parent flower; the parent may be but *slightly* different, but it still differs from its future progeny. The antediluvian ancestors of the present elephant and lizard were, perhaps, the mammoth and the plesiosaurus; why should not the progenitors of our human race have been the "*giants*" of the *Vedas*, the *Völuspa*, and the Book of *Genesis?* While it is positively absurd to believe the "transformation of species" to have taken place according to some of the more materialistic views of the evolutionists, it is but natural to think that each genus, beginning with the molluscs and ending with man, had modified its own primordial and distinctive forms.—"Isis Unveiled," Vol. I., p. 153.

PRELIMINARY NOTES.

ON THE ARCHAIC STANZAS, AND THE FOUR PRE-HISTORIC CONTINENTS.

"Facies totius Universi, quamvis infinitis modis variet,
Manet tamen semper eadem."

—SPINOZA.

THE Stanzas, with the Commentaries thereon, in this Book, the second, are drawn from the same Archaic Records as the Stanzas on Cosmogony in Book I. As far as possible a verbatim translation is given; but some of the Stanzas were too obscure to be understood without explanation. Hence, as was done in Book I., while they are first given in full as they stand, when taken verse by verse with their Commentaries an attempt is made to make them clearer, by words added in brackets, in anticipation of the fuller explanation of the Commentary.

As regards the evolution of mankind, the Secret Doctrine postulates three new propositions, which stand in direct antagonism to modern science as well as to current religious dogmas: it teaches (*a*) the simultaneous evolution of seven human groups on seven different portions of our globe; (*b*) the birth of the *astral*, before the *physical* body: the former being a model for the latter; and (*c*) that man, in this Round, preceded every mammalian—the anthropoids included—in the animal kingdom.*

---

* See Genesis ch. ii., v. 19. Adam is formed in verse 7, and in verse 19 it is said: "Out of the *ground* the Lord God formed *every beast of the field, and every fowl of the air; and brought them unto Adam* to see what he would call them." Thus man was created *before* the animals; for the animals mentioned in chapter i. are the signs of the Zodiac, while the man, "male and female," is not *man*, but the Host of the Sephiroth; FORCES, or Angels, "made in his (God's) image and after his likeness." The Adam, man, is not made in that likeness, nor is it so asserted in the Bible. Moreover, the Second Adam

The Secret Doctrine is not alone in speaking of primeval MEN born simultaneously on the seven divisions of our Globe. In the *Divine "Pymander"* of Hermes we find the same Seven primeval men* evolving from Nature and "Heavenly Man," in the collective sense of the word, namely, from the Creative Spirits; and in the fragments (collected by George Smith) of Chaldean tablets on which is inscribed the Babylonian Legend of Creation, in the first column of the *Cutha* tablet, seven human beings with the faces of ravens (black,s warthy complexions), whom "the (Seven) great gods created," are mentioned. Or, as explained in lines 16 and 18—"In the midst of the Earth they grew up and became great . . . . Seven kings, brothers of the same family." These are the Seven Kings of Edom to whom reference is made in the Kabala; the first race, which was *imperfect, i.e.*, was born before the "balance" (sexes) existed, and which was therefore destroyed. (Zohar, *Siphrah Dzeniouta, Idrah Suta*, 2928, *La Kabbale*, p. 205.) "*Seven Kings*, brethren, appeared and begat children, 6,000 in number were their peoples (Hibbert Lectures, p. 372). The god Nergas (death) destroyed them." "How did he destroy them?" "By bringing into equilibrium (or balance) those who did not yet exist" (*Siphrah Dzeniouta*). They were "destroyed," as a race, by being merged in their own progeny (by exudation); that is to say, the sexless race reincarnated in the bisexual

is esoterically a septenary which represents seven men, or rather groups of men. For the first Adam—the Kadmon—is the synthesis of the *ten* Sephiroth. Of these, the upper triad remains in the Archetypal World as the future "Trinity," while the seven lower Sephiroth create the manifested material world; and *this septennate is the second Adam.* Genesis, and the mysteries upon which it was fabricated, came from Egypt. The "God" of the 1st chapter of Genesis is the *Logos*, and the "Lord God" of the 2nd chapter the Creative *Elohim*—the *lower* powers.

* Thus saith Pymander—"This is the mystery that to this day was hidden. Nature being mingled with the Heavenly man (Elohim, or Dhyanis), brought forth a wonder . . . . *Seven men*, all males and females (Hermaphrodite) . . . according to the nature of the seven Governors"—(Book II. v. 29)—or the seven Hosts of the *Pitris* or Elohim, who projected or created him. This is very clear, but yet, see the interpretations of even our modern theologians, men supposed to be intellectual and learned! In the "*Theological and philosophical works of Hermes Trismegistus, Christian (?) Neoplatonist*," a work compiled by John David Chambers, of Oriel College, Oxford, the translator wonders "for whom these *seven men* are intended?" He solves the difficulty by concluding that, as "the original pattern man (*Adam Kadmon of ch.* i. *Genesis*) was masculine-feminine, the seven may signify the succeeding patriarchs named in Genesis (p. 9) . . . A truly theological way of cutting the Gordian knot.

(potentially); the latter in the Androgynes; these again in the sexual, the later third Race; (for further explanation, *vide infra*). Were the tablets less mutilated, they would be found to contain word for word the same account as given in the archaic records and in Hermes, at least as regards the fundamental facts, if not as regards minute details; for Hermes is a good deal disfigured by mistranslations.

It is quite certain that the seeming supernaturalism of these teachings, although allegorical, is so diametrically opposed to the dead-letter statements of the Bible * as well as to the latest hypotheses of science, that it will evoke passionate denial. The Occultists, however, know that the traditions of Esoteric Philosophy must be the right ones, simply because they are the most logical, and reconcile every difficulty. Besides, we have the Egyptian "*Books of Thoth*," and "*Book of the Dead*," and the Hindu Purânas with the seven Manus, as well as the Chaldeo-Assyrian accounts, whose tiles mention seven primitive men, or Adams, the real meaning of which name may be ascertained through the Kabala. Those who know anything of the Samothracian mysteries will also remember that the generic name of the Kabiri was the "Holy Fires," which created on seven localities of the island of *Electria* (or Samothrace) the "Kabir born of the Holy Lemnos" (the island sacred to *Vulcan*).

According to Pindar (*See "Philosophomena," Miller's edition, p.* 98), this Kabir, whose name was Adamas, was, in the traditions of Lemnos, the type of the primitive man born from the bosom of the Earth. He was the Archetype of the first males in the order of generation, and was one of the seven autochthonous ancestors or progenitors of mankind (*ibid, p.* 108). If, while coupling with this the fact that Samothrace was colonised by the Phoenicians, and before them by the mysterious Pelasgians who came from the East, one remembers also the identity of the *mystery* gods of the Phoenicians, Chaldeans, and Israelites, it will be easy to discover whence came also the confused account of the Noachian deluge. It has become undeniable of late that the Jews, who obtained their primitive ideas about creation from Moses, who had them from

* As it is now asserted that the Chaldean tablets, which give the allegorical description of Creation, the Fall, and the Flood, even to the legend of the Tower of Babel, were written "before the time of Moses" *(See G. Smith's "Chaldean Account of Genesis," p.* 86), how can the Pentateuch be called a *revelation?* It is simply another version of the same story.

the Egyptians, compiled their Genesis and first Cosmogonic traditions—when these were rewritten by Ezra and others—from the Chaldeo-Akkadian account. It is, therefore, sufficient to examine the Babylonian and Assyrian cuneiform and other inscriptions to find also therein, scattered here and there, not only the original meaning of the name Adam, Admi, or Adami,* but also the creation of seven Adams or roots of men, born of Mother Earth, physically, and of the *divine fire* of the progenitors, spiritually or astrally. The Assyriologists, ignorant of the esoteric teachings, could hardly be expected to pay any greater attention to the mysterious and ever-recurring number seven on the Babylonian cylinders, than they paid to it on finding the same in Genesis and the Bible. Yet the number of the ancestral spirits and their seven groups of human progeny are there, notwithstanding the dilapidated condition of the fragments, as plainly as they are to be found in "*Pymander*" and in the "*Book of the Concealed Mystery*" of the Kabala. In the latter Adam Kadmon is the Sephirothal TREE, as also the "Tree of the Knowledge of Good and Evil." And that "*Tree*," says verse 32, "hath around it seven columns," or palaces, of the seven creative Angels operating in the spheres of the seven planets on our Globe. As Adam Kadmon is a *collective* name, so also is the name of the man Adam. Says George Smith in his "*Chaldean Account of Genesis*":—

"The word Adam used in these legends for the first human being is evidently *not a proper name, but is only used as a term for mankind.* Adam appears as a proper name in Genesis, but certainly in some passages is only used in the same sense as the Assyrian word" (*p.* 86).

Moreover, neither the Chaldean nor the Biblical deluge (the stories of Xisuthrus and Noah) is based on the universal or even on the Atlantean deluges, recorded in the Indian allegory of Vaivaswata Manu. They are the *exoteric allegories based on the esoteric mysteries* of Samothrace. If the older Chaldees knew the esoteric truth concealed in the Purânic legends, the other nations were aware only of the Samothracian mystery, and allegorised it. They adapted it to their astronomical and anthropological, or rather phallic, notions. Samothrace is known *historically* to have been famous in antiquity for a deluge, which submerged the country and reached the top of the highest mountains; an event which happened before the age of the Argonauts. It was overflowed very

* *Vide* § "Adam-Adami," in Part II. of this volume.

suddenly by the waters of the Euxine, regarded up to that time as a lake.* But the Israelites had, moreover, another legend upon which to base their allegory: the "deluge," that transformed the present Gobi Desert into a sea *for the last time*, some 10 or 12,000 years ago, and which drove many Noahs and their families on to the surrounding mountains. As the Babylonian accounts are now only restored from hundreds of thousands of broken fragments (the mound of *Kouyunjik* alone having yielded to Layard's excavations over twenty thousand fragments of inscriptions), the proofs here cited are comparatively scanty; yet such as they are, they corroborate almost every one of our teachings, certainly three, at least. These are:—

(1.) That the race which was the first to fall into generation was a *dark Race (Zalmat Gaguadi)*, which they call the *Adami* or dark Race, and that *Sarku*, or the light Race, remained pure for a long while subsequently.

(2.) That the Babylonians recognised *two principal Races* at the time of the Fall, the Race of the Gods (the Ethereal *doubles of the Pitris*), having preceded these two. This is Sir H. Rawlinson's opinion. These "Races" are our second and third Root-races.

(3) That these seven Gods, each of whom created a *man*, or group of men, were "the gods *imprisoned* or incarnated." These gods were: the god *Zi;* the god *Ziku* (noble life, Director of purity); the god *Mirku* (noble crown) "Saviour from death of the gods" (later on) imprisoned, and the creator of "the dark Race which his hand has made;" the god *Libzu* "wise among the gods"; the god *Nissi* . . . . and the god *Suhhab;* and *Hea* or *Sa*, their synthesis, the god of wisdom and of the Deep, identified with Oannes-Dagon, at the time of the fall, and called (collectively) the Demiurge, or Creator. (*See Chaldean Account Genesis*, p. 82.)

There are two "Creations" so called, in the Babylonian fragments, and *Genesis* having adhered to this, one finds its first two chapters distinguished as the Elohite and the Jehovite creations. Their proper order, however, is not preserved in these or in any other exoteric accounts. Now these "Creations," according to the occult teachings, refer respectively to the formation of the primordial seven *men* by the progenitors (the Pitris, or Elohim): and to that of the human groups after the fall.

* See Pliny, 4, c. 12; Strabo, 10; Herodotus, 7, c. 108; Pausanias, 7, c. 4, etc.

All this will be examined in the light of science and comparisons drawn from the scriptures of all the ancient nations, the Bible included, as we proceed. Meanwhile, before we turn to the *Anthropogenesis* of the prehistoric Races, it may be useful to agree upon the names to be given to the Continents on which the four great Races, which preceded our *Adamic* Race, were born, lived, and died. Their archaic and esoteric names were many, and varied with the language of the nationality which mentioned them in its annals and scriptures. That which in the Vendidad, for instance, is referred to as Airyanem Vaêgo (*see Bund.* 79, 12) wherein was born the original Zoroaster,* is called in the Purânic literature "Sveta-Dwipa," "Mount Meru," the abode of Vishnu, etc., etc.; and in the Secret Doctrine is simply named the land of the "Gods" under their chiefs the "Spirits of this Planet."

Therefore, in view of the possible, and even very probable confusion, that may arise, it is considered more convenient to adopt, for each of the four Continents constantly referred to, a name more familiar to the cultured reader. It is proposed, then, to call the first continent, or rather the first *terra firma* on which the first Race was evolved by the divine progenitors:—

I. "The Imperishable Sacred Land."

The reasons for this name are explained as follows: This "Sacred Land"—of which more later on—is stated never to have shared the fate of the other continents; because it is the only one whose destiny it is to last from the beginning to the end of the Manvantara throughout each Round. It is the cradle of the first man and the dwelling of the last *divine* mortal, chosen as a *Sishta* for the future seed of humanity. Of this mysterious and sacred land very little can be said, except, perhaps, according to a poetical expression in one of the Commentaries, that the "pole-star has its watchful eye upon it, from the dawn to the close of the twilight of 'a day' of the GREAT BREATH." †

---

* By "original" we mean the "Amshaspend," called "Zarathustra, the lord and ruler of the Vara made by Yima in that land." There were several Zarathustra or Zertusts, the Dabistan alone enumerating thirteen; but these were all the reincarnations of the first one. The last Zoroaster was the founder of the Fire temple of Azareksh and the writer of the works on the primeval sacred Magian religion destroyed by Alexander.

† In India called "The Day of Brahmâ."

II. The "HYPERBOREAN" will be the name chosen for the Second Continent, the land which stretched out its promontories southward and westward from the North Pole to receive the Second Race, and comprised the whole of what is now known as Northern Asia. Such was the name given by the oldest Greeks to the far-off and mysterious region, whither their tradition made Apollo the "Hyperborean" travel every year. *Astronomically*, Apollo is of course the Sun, who, abandoning his Hellenic sanctuaries, loved to visit annually his far-away country, where the Sun was said never to set for one half of the year. Εγγὺς γὰρ νυκτός τε καὶ ἤματός εἰσι κέλευθοι, says a verse in the *Odyssey* (x. 86).

But *historically*, or better, perhaps, ethnologically and geologically, the meaning is different. The land of the Hyperboreans, the country that extended beyond Boreas, the frozen-hearted god of snows and hurricanes, who loved to slumber heavily on the chain of Mount Riphaeus, was neither an ideal country, as surmised by the mythologists, nor yet a land in the neighbourhood of Scythia and the Danube.* It was a real Continent, a *bonâ-fide* land which knew no winter in those early days, nor have its sorry remains more than one night and day during the year, even now. The nocturnal shadows never fall upon it, said the Greeks; for it is the *land of the Gods*, the favourite abode of Apollo, the god of light, and its inhabitants are his beloved priests and servants. This may be regarded as poetised *fiction* now; but it was poetised *truth* then.

III. The third Continent, we propose to call "Lemuria." The name is an invention, or an idea, of Mr. P. L. Sclater, who asserted, between 1850 and 1860, on zoological grounds the actual existence, in prehistoric times, of a Continent which he showed to have extended from Madagascar to Ceylon and Sumatra. It included some portions of what is now Africa; but otherwise this gigantic Continent, which stretched from the Indian ocean to Australia, has now wholly disappeared beneath the waters of the Pacific, leaving here and there only some of its highland tops which are now islands. Mr. A. R. Wallace, the naturalist, "extends the Australia of tertiary periods to New Guinea and the Solomon Islands, and perhaps to Fiji;" and from its Marsupial types he infers "a connection with the Northern Continent during the

---

* See Volcker, "Mythological Geography," pp. 145 to 170.

Secondary period," writes Mr. C. Gould in "*Mythical Monsters*," p. 47. The subject is treated at length elsewhere.*

IV. "Atlantis" is the Fourth Continent. It would be the first historical land, were the traditions of the ancients to receive more attention than they have hitherto. The famous island of Plato of that name was but a fragment of this great Continent. (*See* "*Esoteric Buddhism*.")

V. The Fifth Continent was America; but, as it is situated at the Antipodes, it is Europe and Asia Minor, almost coeval with it, which are generally referred to by the Indo-Aryan Occultists as the fifth. If their teaching followed the appearance of the Continents in their geological and geographical order, then this classification would have to be altered. But as the sequence of the Continents is made to follow the order of evolution of the Races, from the first to the fifth, our Aryan Root-race, Europe must be called the fifth great Continent. The Secret Doctrine takes no account of islands and peninsulas, nor does it follow the modern geographical distribution of land and sea. Since the day of its earliest teachings and the destruction of the great Atlantis, the face of the earth has changed more than once. There was a time when the delta of Egypt and Northern Africa belonged to Europe, before the formation of the Straits of Gibraltar, and a further upheaval of the continent, changed entirely the face of the map of Europe. The last serious change occurred some 12,000 years ago,†

* It is to be remarked, however, that Mr. Wallace does not accept Mr. Sclater's idea, and even opposes it. Mr. Sclater supposes a land or continent formerly uniting Africa, Madagascar, and India (but not Australia and India); and Mr. A. R. Wallace shows, in his "*Geographical Distribution of Animals*" and "*Island Life*," that the hypothesis of such a land is quite uncalled for on the alleged zoological grounds. But he admits that a much closer proximity of India and Australia did certainly exist, and at a time so very remote that it was "certainly pre-tertiary," and he adds in a private letter that "no name has been given to this supposed land." Yet the land did exist, and was of course *pre-tertiary*, for "Lemuria" (accepting this name for the third Continent) had perished before Atlantis had fully developed; and the latter sunk and its chief portions had disappeared before the end of the Miocene period.

† One more "coincidence"—

"Now it is proved that in geologically recent times, *this region of North Africa was in fact a peninsula of Spain*, and that its union with Africa (proper) was effected on the North by the rupture of Gibraltar, and on the South by an *upheaval to which the Sahara owes its existence*. The shores of this former sea of Sahara are still marked by the shells and was followed by the submersion of Plato's little Atlantic island, which he calls Atlantis after its parent continent. Geography was part of the mysteries, in days of old. Says the *Zohar* (iii., fol. 10*a*): "These secrets (of land and sea) were divulged *to the men of the secret science*, but not to the geographers."

The claim that physical man was originally a colossal pre-tertiary giant, and that he existed 18,000,000 years ago, must of course appear preposterous to admirers of, and believers in, modern learning. The whole *posse comitatus* of biologists will turn away from the conception of this third race Titan of the Secondary age, a being fit to fight as successfully with the then gigantic monsters of the air, sea, and land, as his forefathers—the ethereal prototype of the Atlantean—had little need to fear that which could not hurt him. The modern anthropologist is quite welcome to laugh at our Titans, as he laughs at the Biblical Adam, and as the theologian laughs at his pithecoid ancestor. The Occultists and their severe critics may feel that they have pretty well mutually squared their accounts by this time. Occult sciences claim less and give more, at all events, than either Darwinian Anthropology or Biblical Theology.

Nor ought the Esoteric Chronology to frighten any one; for, with regard to figures, the greatest authorities of the day are as fickle and as uncertain as the Mediterranean wave. As regards the duration of the geological periods alone, the learned men of the Royal Society are all hopelessly at sea, and jump from one million to five hundred millions of years with the utmost ease, as will be seen more than once during this comparison.

Take one instance for our present purpose—the calculations of Mr. Croll. Whether, according to this authority, 2,500,000 years represent the time since the beginning of the tertiary age, or the Eocene period, as an American geologist makes him say;* or whether again Mr. Croll "allows fifteen millions since the beginning of the Eocene period," as quoted by an English geologist,† both sets of figures cover the claims

---

of the same Gastropoda that live on the shores of the Mediterranean." (Prof. Oscas Schmidt, "*Doctrine of Descent and Darwinism*," p. 244.)

* A. Winchell, Professor of Geology, "*World-Life*," p. 369.

† Mr. Charles Gould, late Geological surveyor of Tasmania, in "*Mythical Monsters*," p. 84.

made by the Secret Doctrine.* For assigning as the latter does from four to five million years between the incipient and the final evolution of the Fourth Root-Race, on the Lemuro-Atlantean Continents; one million years for the Fifth, or Aryan Race, to the present date; and about 850,000 since the submersion of the last large peninsula of the great Atlantis—all this may have easily taken place within the 15,000,000 years conceded by Mr. Croll to the Tertiary Age. But, *chronologically* speaking, the duration of the period is of secondary importance, as we have, after all, certain American scientists to fall back upon. These gentlemen, unmoved by the fact that their assertions are called not only dubious but absurd, yet maintain that man existed so far back as in the Secondary Age. They have found human footprints on rocks of that formation; and furthermore, M. de Quatrefages finds no valid *scientific* reason why man should not have existed during the Secondary Age.

The "Ages" and periods in geology are, in sober truth, purely conventional terms, as they are still hardly delineated, and, moreover,

---

* Sir Charles Lyell, who is credited with having "*happily* invented the terms Eocene, Miocene, and Pliocene," to mark the three divisions of the Tertiary age, ought really to have settled upon some approximate age for his "Mind-offspring." Having left the duration of these periods, however, to the speculations of specialists, the greatest confusion and perplexity are the result of that happy thought. It seems like a hopeless task to quote one set of figures from one work, without the risk of finding it contradicted by the same Author in an earlier or a subsequent volume. Sir W. Thomson, one of the most eminent among the modern authorities, has changed, about half-a-dozen times, his opinion upon the age of the Sun and the date of the consolidation of the Earth's crust. In Thomson and Tait's "*Natural Philosophy*," one finds only ten million years allowed, since the time when the temperature of the Earth permitted vegetable life to appear on it; (*App. D et seq. also Trans. Roy. Soc. Edin.* xxiii, *Pt.* 1, 157, 1862, where 847 is cancelled). Mr. Darwin gives Sir W. Thomson's estimate as "a minimum of 98 and a maximum of 200 millions of years since the consolidation of the crust" (See Ch. Gould). In the same work (*Nat. Phil.*) 80 millions are given from the time of incipient incrustation to the present state of the world. And in his last lecture, as shown elsewhere, Sir W. Thomson declares (1887) that the Sun is not older than 15 *millions* of years! Meanwhile, basing his arguments as to the limits to the age of the Sun's heat, on figures previously established by Sir W. Thomson, Mr. Croll allows 60 *millions* of years since the beginning of the Cambrian period. This is hopeful for the lovers of *exact* knowledge. Thus, whatever figures are given by Occult Science, they are sure to be corroborated by those of some one among the modern men of Science who are considered as authorities.

no two geologists or naturalists agree as to the figures. Thus, there is a wide margin for choice offered to the Occultist by the learned fraternity. Shall we take for one of our supports Mr. T. Mellard Reade? This gentleman, in a paper on "Limestone as an Index of Geological Time," read by him in 1878 before the Royal Society, claims that the *minimum* time required for the formation of the sedimentary *strata* and the elimination of the calcareous matter is in round numbers 600 million years (*See "Proceedings of Royal Society," London*, Vol. XXVIII., p. 281); or shall we ask support for our chronology from Mr. Darwin's works, wherein he demands for the organic transformations according to his theory from 300 to 500 million years? Sir C. Lyell and Prof. Houghton were satisfied with placing the beginning of the Cambrian Age at 200 and 240 millions of years back respectively. Geologists and zoologists claim the maximum time, though Mr. Huxley, at one time, placed the beginning of the incrustation of the earth 1,000 million years ago, and would not surrender a millenium of it.

But the main point for us lies not in the agreement or disagreement of the Naturalists as to the duration of geological periods, but rather in their perfect accord on one point, for a wonder, and this a very important one. They all agree that during "The Miocene Age"—whether one or ten million years ago—Greenland and even Spitzbergen, the remnants of our Second or Hyperborean Continent, "had *almost a tropical climate*." Now the pre-Homeric Greeks had preserved a vivid tradition of this "Land of the Eternal Sun," whither their Apollo journeyed yearly. "During the Miocene Age, Greenland (in N. Lat. 70°) developed an abundance of trees, such as the Yew, the Redwood, the Sequoia, allied to the Californian species, Beeches, Planes, Willows, Oaks, Poplars and Walnuts, as well as a Magnolia and a Zamia," says Science; in short Greenland had Southern plants unknown to Northern regions.

And now this natural question rises. If the Greeks knew, in the days of Homer, of a Hyperborean land, *i.e.*, a blessed land beyond the reach of Boreas, the god of winter and of the hurricane, an ideal region which the later Greeks and their classics have vainly tried to locate by searching for it beyond Scythia, a country where nights were short and days long, and beyond that land a country where the sun never set and the palm grew freely—if they knew of all this, who then told them of it? In their day, and for ages previously, Greenland must certainly have been already covered with perpetual snows, with never-thawing ice, just as it is now. Everything tends to show that the land of the short nights and the long days was Norway or Scandinavia, *beyond* which was the blessed land of eternal light and summer ; and to know of this, their tradition must have descended to the Greeks from some people more ancient than themselves, who were acquainted with those climatic details of which the Greeks themselves could know nothing. Even in our day, science suspects beyond the Polar seas, at the very circle of the Arctic Pole, the existence of a sea which never freezes and a continent which is ever green. The archaic teachings, and likewise the Purânas—for one who understands the allegories of the latter—contain the same statements. Suffice, then, to us the strong probability that a people, now unknown to history, lived during the Miocene period of modern science, at a time when Greenland was an almost tropical land.

NOTE. The reader is requested to bear in mind that the first and the following sections are not strictly consecutive in order of time. In the first Section the Stanzas which form the skeleton of the exposition are given, and certain important points commented upon and explained. In the subsequent sections various additional details are gathered, and a fuller explanation of the subject is attempted.

BOOK II.—PART I.

ANTHROPOGENESIS.

STANZAS TRANSLATED WITH COMMENTARIES

FROM THE

SECRET BOOK OF DZYAN.

In primeval times, a maiden,
Beauteous Daughter of the Ether,
Passed for ages her existence
In the great expanse of Heaven,

. . . .

Seven hundred years she wandered,
Seven hundred years she laboured,
Ere her first-born was delivered.

. . . .

Ere a beauteous duck descending,
Hastens toward the water-mother.

. . . .

Lightly on the knee she settles,
Finds a nesting-place befitting,
Where to lay her eggs in safety,
Lays her eggs within, at pleasure,
Six, the golden eggs she lays them,
Then a *Seventh*, an egg of iron . . . . ."

(*Kalevala*, *Rune* I.)

ANTHROPOGENESIS IN THE SECRET VOLUME.

(VERBATIM EXTRACTS.*)

I.

1. THE LHA WHICH TURNS THE FOURTH IS SUBSERVIENT TO THE LHA OF THE SEVEN, THEY WHO REVOLVE DRIVING THEIR CHARIOTS AROUND THEIR LORD, THE ONE EYE. HIS BREATH GAVE LIFE TO THE SEVEN; IT GAVE LIFE TO THE FIRST.

2. SAID THE EARTH:—"LORD OF THE SHINING FACE; MY HOUSE IS EMPTY . . . . SEND THY SONS TO PEOPLE THIS WHEEL. THOU HAST SENT THY SEVEN SONS TO THE LORD OF WISDOM. SEVEN TIMES DOTH HE SEE THEE NEARER TO HIMSELF, SEVEN TIMES MORE DOTH HE FEEL THEE. THOU HAST FORBIDDEN THY SERVANTS, THE SMALL RINGS, TO CATCH THY LIGHT AND HEAT, THY GREAT BOUNTY TO INTERCEPT ON ITS PASSAGE. SEND NOW TO THY SERVANT THE SAME."

3. SAID THE "LORD OF THE SHINING FACE":—"I SHALL SEND THEE A FIRE WHEN THY WORK IS COMMENCED. RAISE THY VOICE TO OTHER LOKAS; APPLY TO THY FATHER, THE LORD OF THE LOTUS, FOR HIS SONS . . . . THY PEOPLE SHALL BE UNDER THE RULE OF THE FATHERS. THY MEN SHALL BE MORTALS. THE MEN OF THE LORD OF WISDOM, NOT THE LUNAR SONS, ARE IMMORTAL. CEASE THY COMPLAINTS. THY SEVEN SKINS ARE YET ON THEE . . . . THOU ART NOT READY. THY MEN ARE NOT READY."

4. AFTER GREAT THROES SHE CAST OFF HER OLD THREE AND PUT ON HER NEW SEVEN SKINS, AND STOOD IN HER FIRST ONE.

II.

5. THE WHEEL WHIRLED FOR THIRTY CRORES MORE. IT CONSTRUCTED RUPAS: SOFT STONES THAT HARDENED; HARD PLANTS THAT SOFTENED. VISIBLE FROM INVISIBLE, INSECTS AND SMALL LIVES. SHE SHOOK THEM OFF HER BACK WHENEVER THEY OVERRAN THE MOTHER.

* Only forty-nine Slokas out of several hundred are here given. Not every verse is translated verbatim. A periphrasis is sometimes used for the sake of clearness and intelligibility, where a literal translation would be quite unintelligible.

. . . . After thirty crores she turned round. She lay on her back; on her side . . . She would call no sons of Heaven, she would ask no sons of Wisdom. She created from her own bosom. She evolved water-men, terrible and bad.

6. The water-men terrible and bad she herself created from the remains of others, from the dross and slime of her first, second, and third, she formed them. The Dhyani came and looked—The Dhyani from the bright Father-mother, from the white regions they came, from the abodes of the immortal mortals.

7. Displeased they were. Our flesh is not there. No fit rupas for our brothers of the fifth. No dwellings for the lives. Pure waters, not turbid, they must drink. Let us dry them.

8. The flames came. The fires with the sparks; the night fires and the day fires. They dried out the turbid dark waters. With their heat they quenched them. The Lhas of the High, the Lhamayin of below, came. They slew the forms which were two- and four-faced. They fought the goat-men, and the dog-headed men, and the men with fishes' bodies.

9. Mother-water, the great sea, wept. She arose, she disappeared in the moon which had lifted her, which had given her birth.

10. When they were destroyed, Mother-earth remained bare. She asked to be dried.

III.

11. The Lord of the Lords came. From her body he separated the waters, and that was Heaven above, the first Heaven.

12. The great Chohans called the Lords of the Moon, of the airy bodies. "Bring forth men, men of your nature. Give them their forms within. She will build coverings without. Males-females will they be. Lords of the Flame also . . . ."

13. They went each on his allotted land: seven of them each on his lot. The Lords of the Flame remain behind. They would not go, they would not create.

IV.

14. THE SEVEN HOSTS, THE "WILL-BORN LORDS," PROPELLED BY THE SPIRIT OF LIFE-GIVING, SEPARATE MEN FROM THEMSELVES, EACH ON HIS OWN ZONE.

15. SEVEN TIMES SEVEN SHADOWS OF FUTURE MEN WERE BORN, EACH OF HIS OWN COLOUR AND KIND. EACH INFERIOR TO HIS FATHER. THE FATHERS, THE BONELESS, COULD GIVE NO LIFE TO BEINGS WITH BONES. THEIR PROGENY WERE BHÛTA, WITH NEITHER FORM NOR MIND. THEREFORE THEY ARE CALLED THE CHHAYA.

16. HOW ARE THE MANUSHYA BORN? THE MANUS WITH MINDS, HOW ARE THEY MADE? THE FATHERS CALLED TO THEIR HELP THEIR OWN FIRE; WHICH IS THE FIRE THAT BURNS IN EARTH. THE SPIRIT OF THE EARTH CALLED TO HIS HELP THE SOLAR FIRE. THESE THREE PRODUCED IN THEIR JOINT EFFORTS A GOOD RUPA. IT COULD STAND WALK, RUN, RECLINE, OR FLY. YET IT WAS STILL BUT A CHHAYA, A SHADOW WITH NO SENSE . . . .

17. THE BREATH NEEDED A FORM; THE FATHERS GAVE IT. THE BREATH NEEDED A GROSS BODY; THE EARTH MOULDED IT. THE BREATH NEEDED THE SPIRIT OF LIFE; THE SOLAR LHAS BREATHED IT INTO ITS FORM. THE BREATH NEEDED A MIRROR OF ITS BODY; "WE GAVE IT OUR OWN," SAID THE DHYANIS. THE BREATH NEEDED A VEHICLE OF DESIRES; "IT HAS IT," SAID THE DRAINER OF WATERS. BUT BREATH NEEDS A MIND TO EMBRACE THE UNIVERSE; "WE CANNOT GIVE THAT," SAID THE FATHERS. "I NEVER HAD IT," SAID THE SPIRIT OF THE EARTH. "THE FORM WOULD BE CONSUMED WERE I TO GIVE IT MINE." SAID THE GREAT FIRE . . . . MAN REMAINED AN EMPTY SENSELESS BHÛTA . . . . THUS HAVE THE BONELESS GIVEN LIFE TO THOSE WHO BECAME MEN WITH BONES IN THE THIRD.

V.

18. THE FIRST WERE THE SONS OF YOGA. THEIR SONS THE CHILDREN OF THE YELLOW FATHER AND THE WHITE MOTHER.

19. THE SECOND RACE WAS THE PRODUCT BY BUDDING AND

expansion, the A-Sexual from the Sexless.* Thus was, O Lanoo, the Second Race produced.

20. Their fathers were the self-born. The self-born, the Chhaya from the brilliant bodies of the Lords, the Fathers, the Sons of Twilight.

21. When the Race became old, the old waters mixed with the fresher waters. When its drops became turbid, they vanished and disappeared in the new stream, in the hot stream of life. The outer of the first became the inner of the second. The old Wing became the new Shadow, and the Shadow of the Wing.

VI.

22. Then the second evolved the Egg-born, the third. The sweat grew, its drops grew, and the drops became hard and round. The Sun warmed it; the Moon cooled and shaped it; the wind fed it until its ripeness. The white swan from the starry vault overshadowed the big drop. The egg of the future race, the Man-swan of the later third. First male-female, then man and woman.

23. The self-born were the Chhayas: the Shadows from the bodies of the Sons of Twilight.

VII.

24. The Sons of Wisdom, the Sons of Night, ready for re-birth, came down, they saw the vile forms of the First Third, "We can choose," said the Lords, "we have wisdom." Some entered the Chhaya. Some projected the Spark. Some deferred till the Fourth. From their own Rupa they filled the Kama. Those who entered became Arhats. Those who received but a spark, remained destitute of knowledge; the spark burned low. The third remained mind-less. Their Jivas were not

* The idea and the spirit of the sentence is here given, as a verbal translation would convey very little to the reader.

READY. THESE WERE SET APART AMONG THE SEVEN. THEY BECAME NARROW-HEADED. THE THIRD WERE READY. "IN THESE SHALL WE DWELL," SAID THE LORDS OF THE FLAME.

25. HOW DID THE MANÂSA, THE SONS OF WISDOM, ACT? THEY REJECTED THE SELF-BORN. THEY ARE NOT READY. THEY SPURNED THE SWEAT-BORN. THEY ARE NOT QUITE READY. THEY WOULD NOT ENTER THE FIRST EGG-BORN.

26. WHEN THE SWEAT-BORN PRODUCED THE EGG-BORN, THE TWOFOLD AND THE MIGHTY, THE POWERFUL WITH BONES, THE LORDS OF WISDOM SAID: "NOW SHALL WE CREATE."

27. THE THIRD RACE BECAME THE VAHAN OF THE LORDS OF WISDOM. IT CREATED "SONS OF WILL AND YOGA," BY KRIYASAKTI IT CREATED THEM, THE HOLY FATHERS, ANCESTORS OF THE ARHATS. .

VIII.

28. FROM THE DROPS OF SWEAT; FROM THE RESIDUE OF THE SUB STANCE; MATTER FROM DEAD BODIES OF MEN AND ANIMALS OF THE WHEEL BEFORE; AND FROM CAST-OFF DUST, THE FIRST ANIMALS WERE PRODUCED.

29. ANIMALS WITH BONES, DRAGONS OF THE DEEP, AND FLYING SARPAS WERE ADDED TO THE CREEPING THINGS. THEY THAT CREEP ON THE GROUND GOT WINGS. THEY OF THE LONG NECKS IN THE WATER BECAME THE PROGENITORS OF THE FOWLS OF THE AIR.

30. DURING THE THIRD RACE THE BONELESS ANIMALS GREW AND CHANGED: THEY BECAME ANIMALS WITH BONES, THEIR CHHAYAS BECAME SOLID.

31. THE ANIMALS SEPARATED THE FIRST. THEY BEGAN TO BREED. THE TWO-FOLD MAN SEPARATED ALSO. HE SAID: "LET US AS THEY; LET US UNITE AND MAKE CREATURES." THEY DID.

32. AND THOSE WHICH HAD NO SPARK TOOK HUGE SHE-ANIMALS UNTO THEM. THEY BEGAT UPON THEM DUMB RACES. DUMB THEY WERE THEMSELVES. BUT THEIR TONGUES UNTIED. THE TONGUES OF THEIR PROGENY REMAINED STILL. MONSTERS THEY BRED. A RACE OF CROOKED RED-HAIR-COVERED MONSTERS GOING ON ALL FOURS. A DUMB RACE TO KEEP THE SHAME UNTOLD.

IX.

33. Seeing which, the Lhas who had not built men, wept, saying :—

34. "The Amanâsa have defiled our future abodes. This is Karma. Let us dwell in the others. Let us teach them better, lest worse should happen. They did . . . .

35. Then all men became endowed with Manas. They saw the sin of the mindless.

36. The Fourth Race developed speech.

37. The One became Two; also all the living and creeping things that were still one, giant fish-birds and serpents with shell-heads.

X.

38. Thus two by two on the seven zones, the Third Race gave birth to the Fourth-Race men; the gods became no-gods; the sura became a-sura.

39. The first, on every zone, was moon-coloured; the second yellow like gold; the third red; the fourth brown, which became black with sin. The first seven human shoots were all of one complexion. The next seven began mixing.

40. Then the Fourth became tall with pride. We are the kings, it was said; we are the gods.

41. They took wives fair to look upon. Wives from the mindless, the narrow-headed. They bred monsters. Wicked demons, male and female, also Khado (dakini), with little minds.

42. They built temples for the human body. Male and female they worshipped. Then the Third Eye acted no longer.

XI.

43. They built huge cities. Of rare earths and metals they built, and out of the fires vomited, out of the white stone of

THE MOUNTAINS AND OF THE BLACK STONE, THEY CUT THEIR OWN IMAGES IN THEIR SIZE AND LIKENESS, AND WORSHIPPED THEM.

44. THEY BUILT GREAT IMAGES NINE YATIS HIGH, THE SIZE OF THEIR BODIES. INNER FIRES HAD DESTROYED THE LAND OF THEIR FATHERS. THE WATER THREATENED THE FOURTH.

45. THE FIRST GREAT WATERS CAME. THEY SWALLOWED THE SEVEN GREAT ISLANDS.

46. ALL HOLY SAVED, THE UNHOLY DESTROYED. WITH THEM MOST OF THE HUGE ANIMALS, PRODUCED FROM THE SWEAT OF THE EARTH.

XII.

47. FEW MEN REMAINED: SOME YELLOW, SOME BROWN AND BLACK, AND SOME RED REMAINED. THE MOON-COLOURED WERE GONE FOREVER.

48. THE FIFTH PRODUCED FROM THE HOLY STOCK REMAINED; IT WAS RULED OVER BY THE FIRST DIVINE KINGS.

49. . . . . WHO RE-DESCENDED, WHO MADE PEACE WITH THE FIFTH, WHO TAUGHT AND INSTRUCTED IT. . . . . .

200.

§ XXIV

The Cross & the Pythagorean Decade

The early gnostics claimed that their Science, the Gnosis, rested on a square, the angles of which represented respectively Sige, (Silence), Bathos (depth), Nous (Spiritual Soul or Mind) and Aletheia (Truth.

It is they who were the first to introduce & reveal to the world that which had remained concealed from the profane for long ages, buried as it was under the impenetrable veil of the secrecy of Initiation, & enacted only during the Inner mysteries: namely the Tau in the shape of a Procrustean bed, and Christos as incarnating in Chrestos, he who became for certain purposes a willing candidate for a series of

Portion of *Secret Doctrine* manuscript page, II:573. (TS Archives, Pasadena)

CONCLUSION.

Space forbids us to say anything more, and this part of the "Secret Doctrine" has to be closed. The forty-nine Stanzas and the few fragments from the Commentaries just given are all that can be published in these volumes. These, with some still older records—to which none but the highest Initiates have access—and a whole library of comments, glossaries, and explanations, form the synopsis of Man's genesis.

It is from the Commentaries that we have hitherto quoted and tried to explain the hidden meaning of some of the allegories, thus showing the true views of esoteric antiquity upon geology, anthropology, and even ethnology. We will endeavour in the Part which follows, to establish a still closer metaphysical connection between the earliest races and their Creators, the *divine* men from other worlds; accompanying the statements proffered with the most important demonstrations of the same in esoteric Astronomy and Symbolism.

In Volume III. of this work (the said volume and the IVth being almost ready) a brief history of all the great adepts known to the ancients and the moderns in their chronological order will be given, as also a bird's eye view of the Mysteries, their birth, growth, decay, and final death—in Europe. This could not find room in the present work. Volume IV. will be almost entirely devoted to Occult teachings.

The duration of the periods that separate, in space and time, the Fourth from the Fifth Race—in the historical * or even the legendary beginnings of the latter—is too tremendous for us to offer, even to a Theosophist, any more detailed accounts of them. During the course of the post-diluvian ages—marked at certain periodical epochs by the most terrible cataclysms—too many races and nations were born, and have disappeared almost without leaving a trace, for any one to offer any description of the slightest value concerning them. Whether the Masters of Wisdom have a consecutive and full history of our race from its incipient stage down to the present times; whether they possess the uninterrupted record of man since he became the complete physical being, and became thereby the king of the animals and master on this earth—is not for the writer to say. Most probably they have,

* The word "historical" is used, because, although historians have dwarfed almost absurdly the dates that separate certain events from our modern day, nevertheless, once that they are known and accepted, they belong to history. Thus the Trojan War *is* an historical event; and though even less than 1,000 years B.C. is the date assigned to it, yet in truth it is nearer 6,000 than 5,000 years B.C.

and such is our own personal conviction. But if so, this knowledge is only for the *highest* Initiates, who do not take their students into their confidence. The writer can, therefore, give but what she has herself been taught, and no more.

But even this will appear to the profane reader rather as a weird, fantastic dream, than as a possible reality.

This is only natural and as it should be, since for years such was the impression made upon the humble writer of these pages herself. Born and bred in European, matter-of-fact and presumably civilized countries, she assimilated the foregoing with the utmost difficulty. But there are proofs of a certain character which become irrefutable and are undeniable in the long run, to every earnest and unprejudiced mind. For a series of years such were offered to her, and now she has the full certitude that our present globe and its human races must have been born, grown and developed in this, and in no other way.

But this is the personal view of the writer; and her orthodoxy cannot be expected to have any more weight than any other "doxy," in the eyes of those to whom every fresh theory is heterodox until otherwise proved. Therefore are we Occultists fully prepared for such questions as these: "How does one know that the writer has not invented the whole scheme? And supposing *she* has not, how can one tell that the whole of the foregoing, as given in the Stanzas, is not the product of the imagination of the ancients? How could they have preserved the records of such an immense, such an incredible antiquity?"

The answer that the history of this world since its formation and to its end "is written in the stars," *i.e.*, is recorded in the Zodiac and the Universal Symbolism whose keys are in the keeping of the Initiates, will hardly satisfy the doubters. The antiquity of the Zodiac in Egypt is much doubted, and it is denied point-blank with regard to India. "Your conclusions are often excellent, but your premises are always doubtful," the writer was once told by a profane friend. To this, the answer came that it was one point, at least, gained on the scientific syllogisms. For, with the exception of a few problems from the domain of purely physical science, both the premises and conclusions of the men of Science are as hypothetical as they are almost invariably erroneous. And if they do not so appear to the profane, the reason is simply this: the said profane is very little aware, taking as he does his scientific data on faith, that both premises and conclusions are generally the product of the same brains, which, however learned, are not infallible; a truism demonstrated daily by the shifting and re-shifting of scientific theories and speculations.

However it may be, the records of the temples, Zodiacal and traditional, as well as the ideographic records of the East, as read by the adepts of the Sacred Science and Vidya, are not a whit more doubtful than the so-called ancient history of the European nations, now edited, corrected, and amplified by half a century of archæological discoveries, and the very problematical readings of the Assyrian tiles, cuneiform fragments, and Egyptian hieroglyphics. So are our data based upon the same readings, in addition to an almost inexhaustible number of Secret works of which Europe knows nothing—*plus* the perfect knowledge by the Initiates of the symbolism of every word so recorded. Some of these records belong to an immense antiquity. Every archæologist and palæontologist is acquainted with the ideographic productions of certain semi-savage tribes, who from time immemorial have aimed at rendering their thoughts symbolically. This is the earliest mode of recording events and ideas. And how old this knowledge is in the human race may be inferred from some signs, evidently ideographic, found on hatchets of the Palæolithic period. The red Indian tribes of America, only a few years ago comparatively speaking, petitioned the President of the United States to grant them possession of four small lakes, the petition being written on the tiny surface of a piece of a fabric, which is covered with barely a dozen representations of animals and birds. (See Lubbock.) The American savages have a number of such different kinds of writing, but not one of our Scientists is yet familiar, or even knows of the early hieroglyphic cypher, still preserved in some Fraternities, and named in Occultism the *Senzar*. Moreover, all those who have decided to regard such modes of writing—*e.g.*, the ideographs of the Red Indians, and even the Chinese characters—as "attempts of the early races of mankind to express their untutored thoughts," will decidedly object to our statement, that writing was invented by the Atlanteans, and not at all by the Phœnicians. Indeed, such a claim as that writing was known to mankind many hundreds of millenniums ago, in the face of the philologists who have decreed that writing was unknown in the days of, and to Pânini, in India, as also to the Greeks in the time of Homer, will be met by general disapprobation, if not with silent scorn. All denial and ridicule notwithstanding, the Occultists will maintain the claim, and simply for this reason: from Bacon down to our modern Royal Society, we have a too long period, full of the most ludicrous mistakes made by Science, to warrant our believing in modern scientific assumptions rather than in the denials of our Teachers. Writing, our scientists say, was unknown to Pânini; and this sage nevertheless composed a grammar which contains 3,996 rules, and is the most perfect of all the grammars that were ever made! Pânini is made out to have lived barely a few centuries B.C., by the most liberal; and the rocks in Iran and Central Asia (whence the philologists and historians show us the ancestors of the same Pânini, the Brahmins, coming into India) are *covered with writing*, two and three thousand years old (12,000, according to some fearless palæontologists).

Writing was an *ars incognita* in the days of Hesiod and Homer, agreeably to Grote, and unknown to the Greeks so late as 770 B.C.; and the Phœnicians who had *invented* it, and knew writing as far back as 1500 B.C., at the earliest,* were living among the Greeks, and elbowing them, all the time! All these scientific and contradictory conclusions disappeared, however, into thin air, when Schliemann discovered (*a*) the site of ancient Troy, whose actual existence had been so long regarded as a fable; and (*b*), excavated on that site earthenware vessels with inscriptions *in characters unknown* to the palæontologists and the all-denying Sanskritists. Who will now deny Troy, or these Archaic inscriptions? As Professor Virchow witnesses:—"I was myself an eye-witness of two such discoveries, and helped to gather the articles together. The slanderers have long since been silenced, who were not ashamed to charge the discoverer with an imposture."† Nor were truthful women spared any more than truthful men. Du Chaillu, Gordon-Cumming, Madame Merian,‡ Bruce, and a host of others were charged with lying.

Madame Merian—says the author of "*Mythical Monsters*," who gives this information in the *Introduction*—was accused of deliberate falsehood in reference to her description of a bird-eating spider nearly two hundred years ago. But now-a-days reliable observers have confirmed it in regard to South America, India, and elsewhere. Audubon was accused by botanists of having invented the yellow water-lily, which he figured in his *Birds of the South* under the name of Nymphæa lutea, and after having lain under the imputation for years, was confirmed at last by the discovery of the long-lost flower in Florida in 1876 (*Pop. Sci. Monthly*, No. 60, April 1877). And, as Audubon was called *a liar* for this, and for his Holiætus Washingtonii,§ so Victor Hugo was ridiculed for . . . . his marvellous word-painting of the devil-fish, and his description of a man becoming its helpless victim. "The thing was derided as an impossibility; yet within a few years were discovered, on the shores of Newfoundland, cuttle fish with arms extending to thirty feet in length, and capable of dragging a good-sized

---

* It is an historical fact that Sanchoniathon compiled and wrote in Phœnician characters—from annals and State documents in the archives of *the older* Phœnician cities—the full record of their religion in 1250 B.C.

† Prof. Virchow, in Appendix 1 to Schliemann's *Ilios*. Murray, 1880.

‡ Gosse writes of the latter: "She is set down a thorough heretic, not at all to be believed, a manufacturer of unsound natural history, an inventor of false facts in science." ("*Romance of Natural History*," p. 227.)

§ Dr. Cover writes: "That famous bird of Washington was a myth; either Audubon was mistaken, or else, as some do not hesitate to affirm, *he lied* about it."

boat beneath the surface; and their action has been reproduced *for centuries past* . . . . by Japanese artists." ("*Mythical Monsters*," p. 11 *Introd.*).

And if Troy was denied, and regarded as a myth; the existence of Herculaneum and Pompeii declared a fiction; the travels of Marco Polo laughed at and called as absurd a fable as one of Baron Münchausen's tales, why should the writer of "Isis Unveiled" and of the "Secret Doctrine" be any better treated? Mr. Charles Gould, the author of the above-cited volume quotes in his excellent work a few lines from Macmillan (1860), which are as true as life, and too much to the point not to be reproduced: "When a naturalist, either by visiting such spots of earth as are still out of the way, or by his good fortune, finds a very queer plant or animal, he is forthwith accused of *inventing* his game. . . . . . As soon as the creature is found to sin against preconception, the great (mis?) guiding Spirit, *a priori* by name, who furnishes philosophers with their omniscience *pro re natâ*, whispers that no such thing *can* be, and forthwith there is a charge of hoax. The heavens themselves have been charged with hoaxes. When Leverrier and Adams predicted a planet by calculation, it was gravely asserted in some quarters that the planet which had been calculated was not *the* planet but another which had clandestinely and improperly got into the neighbourhood of the true body. *The disposition to suspect hoax is stronger than the disposition to hoax.* Who was it that first announced that the classical writings of Greece and Rome were one huge hoax perpetrated by the monks in what the announcer would be as little or less inclined than Dr. Maitland to call the dark ages?" (p. 13).

Thus let it be. No disbeliever who takes the "Secret Doctrine" for a "hoax" is forced or even asked to credit our statements. These have already been proclaimed to be such by certain very clever American journalists before even the work went to press.*

Nor, is it after all, necessary that any one should believe in the Occult Sciences and the old teachings, before one knows anything or even

* So far back as July, 1888, at a time when the MSS. of this work had not yet left my writing table, and the *Secret Doctrine* was utterly unknown to the world, it was already being denounced as a product of my brain and no more. These are the flattering terms in which the *Evening Telegraph* (of America) referred to this still unpublished work in its issue of June 30, 1888: "*Among the fascinating books for July reading* is Mme. Blavatsky's new book on Theosophy . . . (!) the SECRET DOCTRINE. . . . But because she can soar back into the Brahmin ignorance . . . (! ?) . . . *is no proof that everything she says is true.*" And once the prejudiced verdict given on the mistaken notion that my book was out, and that the reviewer had read it, neither of which was or could be the case, now that it is really out the critic will have to support his first statement, whether correct or otherwise, and thus get out of it, probably by a more slashing criticism than ever.

believes in his own soul. No great truth was ever accepted *a priori*. and generally a century or two passed before it began to glimmer in the human consciousness as a possible verity, except in such cases as the positive discovery of the thing claimed as a fact. The truths of to-day are the falsehoods and errors of yesterday, and *vice versâ*. It is only in the XXth century that portions, if not the whole, of the present work will be vindicated.

It is no fact going against our statements, therefore, even if Sir John Evans does affirm that writing was unknown in the stone age. For it may have been unknown during that period in the Fifth Aryan race, and have been perfectly known to the Atlanteans of the Fourth, in the palmy days of their highest civilization. The cycles of the rise and fall of the nations and races are there to account for it.

If told that there have been cases before now of forged pseudographs being palmed off on the credulous, and that our work may be classed with Jacolliot's "Bible in India" (in which, by the way, there are more truths among its errors than are found in the works of orthodox and recognized Orientalists)—the charge and comparison will dismay us very little. We bide our time. Even the famous "Ezour-Veda" of the last century, considered by Voltaire "the most precious gift from the East to the West," and by Max Müller "about the silliest book that can be read," is not altogether without facts and truths in it. The cases when the *a priori* negations of specialists became justified by subsequent corroborations form but an insignificant percentage of those that were fully vindicated by subsequent discoveries, and confirmed to the great dismay of the learned objectors. "Ezour Veda," was a very small bone of contention compared with the triumph of Sir William Jones, Anquetil de Perron, and others in the matter of Sanskrit and its literature. Such facts are recorded by Professor Max Müller himself, who, speaking of the discomfiture of Dugald Stewart and Co. in connection with this, states that "if the facts about Sanskrit were true, Dugald Stewart was too wise not to see that the conclusions drawn from them were inevitable. He therefore denied the reality of such a language as Sanskrit altogether, and wrote his famous essay to prove that Sanskrit had been put together after the model of Greek and Latin, by those arch-forgers and liars, the Brahmans, and that the whole of Sanskrit literature was an imposition" (*Science of Language*, p. 168). The writer is quite willing and feels proud to keep company with these Brahmans, and other *historical* "liars," in the opinion of our modern Dugald Stewarts. She has lived too long, and her experience has been too varied and personal, for her not to know at least something of human nature. "When you doubt, abstain," says the wise Zoroaster, whose prudent aphorism is found corroborated in every case by daily life and experience. Yet, like St. John the Baptist, this sage of the past Ages is found preaching in the desert, in company with a more modern philosopher, namely Bacon, who offers the same priceless bit of practical Wisdom. "In contemplation," he says (in any question of Knowledge, we add), "if a man begin with certainties, he shall end in doubts; but *if he will be content to begin with doubts, he shall end in certainties.*"

With this piece of advice from the father of English Philosophy to the representatives of British scepticism we ought to close the debate, but our theosophical readers are entitled to a final piece of Occult information.

Enough was said to show that evolution in general, events, mankind, and everything else in Nature proceed in cycles. We have spoken of seven Races, five of which have nearly completed their earthly career, and have claimed that every Root-Race, with its sub-races and innumerable family divisions and tribes, was entirely distinct from its preceding and succeeding race. This will be objected to, on the authority of uniform experience in the question of Anthropology, and Ethnology. Man was—save in colour and type, and perhaps a difference in facial peculiarities and cranial capacity—ever the same under every climate and in every part of the world, say the Naturalists: ay, even in stature. This, while maintaining that man descends from the same unknown ancestor as the ape, a claim that is logically impossible without an infinite variation of stature and form, from his first evolution into a biped. The very logical persons who maintain both propositions are welcome to their paradoxical views. Once more we address only those who, doubting the general derivation of myths from "the contemplation of the visible workings of external nature" . . . . think it, "less hard to believe that these wonderful stories of gods and demi-gods, of giants and dwarfs, of dragons and monsters of all descriptions, are transformations, than to believe them to be inventions." It is only such "transformations" in physical nature, as much as in the memory and conceptions of our present mankind, that the Secret Doctrine teaches. It confronts the purely speculative hypotheses of modern Science, based upon the experience and exact observations of barely a few centuries, with the unbroken tradition and records of its Sanctuaries; and brushing away that tissue of cobweb-like theories, spun in the darkness that covers a period of hardly a few millenniums back, and which Europeans call their "History," the Old Science says to us: Listen, now, to my version of the memoirs of Humanity.

The human Races are born one from the other, grow, develop, become old, and die. Their sub-races and nations follow the same rule. If your all-denying modern science and so-called philosophy do not contest that the human family is composed of a variety of well-defined types and races, it is only because the fact is undeniable; no one would say that there was no external difference between an Englishman, an African negro, and a Japanese or Chinaman. On the other hand it is formally denied by most naturalists that *mixed human races*, *i.e.*, the seeds for entirely new races, are any longer formed in our days. But this last is maintained on good grounds by de Quatrefages and some others.

Nevertheless our general proposition will not be accepted. It will be said that whatever forms man has passed through in the long pre-historic Past there are no more changes for him (save certain variations, as at present) in the future. Hence that our Sixth and Seventh Root Races are fictions.

To this it is again answered: How *do you* know? Your experience is limited to a few thousand years, to less than a day in the whole age of Humanity and to the present types of the actual continents and isles of our Fifth Race. How can you tell what will or will not be? Meanwhile, such is the prophecy of the Secret Books and their no uncertain statements.

Since the beginning of the Atlantean Race many million years have passed, yet we find the last of the Atlanteans, still mixed up with the Aryan element, 11,000 years ago. This shows the enormous overlapping of one race over the race which succeeds it, though in character and external type the elder loses its characteristics, and assumes the new features of the younger race. This is proved in all the formations of mixed human races. Now, Occult philosophy teaches that even now, under our very eyes, the new Race and Races are preparing to be formed, and that it is in America that the transformation will take place, and has already silently commenced.

Pure Anglo-Saxons hardly three hundred years ago, the Americans of the United States have already become a nation apart, and, owing to a strong admixture of various nationalities and inter-marriage, almost a race *sui generis*, not only mentally, but also physically. "Every mixed race, when uniform and settled, has been able to play the part of a primary race in fresh crossings," says de Quatrefages. "Mankind, in its present state, has thus been formed, certainly, for the greatest part, by the successive crossing of a number of races *at present undetermined*." ("*The Human Species*," *p.* 274.)

Thus the Americans have become in only three centuries a "primary race," *pro tem.*, before becoming a race apart, and strongly separated from all other now existing races. They are, in short, the germs of the *Sixth* sub-race, and in some few hundred years more, will become most decidedly the pioneers of that race which must succeed to the present European or fifth sub-race, in all its new characteristics. After this, in about 25,000 years, they will launch into preparations for the seventh sub-race ; until, in consequence of cataclysms—the first series of those which must one day destroy Europe, and still later the whole Aryan race (and thus affect both Americas), as also most of the lands directly connected with the confines of our continent and isles—the Sixth Root-Race will have appeared on the stage of our Round. When shall this be? Who knows save the great Masters of Wisdom, perchance, and they are as silent upon the subject as the snow-capped peaks that tower above them. All we know is, that it will silently come into existence; so silently, indeed, that for long millenniums shall its pioneers—the peculiar children who will grow into peculiar men and women—be regarded as anomalous *lusus naturæ*, abnormal oddities physically and mentally. Then, as they increase, and their numbers become with every age greater, one day they will awake to find themselves in a majority. It is the present men who will then begin to be regarded as exceptional mongrels, until these die out in their turn in civilised lands; surviving only in small groups on islands—the mountain peaks of to-day—where they will vegetate, degenerate, and finally die out, perhaps millions of years hence, as the Aztecs have, as the Nyam-Nyam and the dwarfish Moola Koorumba of the Nilghiri Hills are dying. All these are the remnants of once mighty races, the recollection of whose existence has entirely died out of the remembrance of the modern generations, just as we shall vanish from the memory of the Sixth Race Humanity. The Fifth will overlap the Sixth Race for many hundreds of millenniums, changing with it slower than its new successor, still changing in stature, general physique, and mentality, just as the Fourth overlapped our Aryan race, and the Third had overlapped the Atlanteans.

This process of preparation for the Sixth great Race must last throughout the whole sixth and seventh sub-races (*vide supra*, the diagram of the Genealogical Tree of the Fifth Race). But the *last* remnants of the Fifth Continent will not disappear until some time after the birth of the *new* Race; when another and *new* dwelling, the sixth continent, will have appeared above the *new* waters on the face of the globe, so as to receive the new stranger. To it also will emigrate and settle all those who shall be fortunate enough to escape the general disaster. When this shall be—as just said—it is not for the writer to know. Only, as nature no more proceeds by sudden jumps and starts, than man changes suddenly from a child into a mature man, the final cataclysm will be preceded by many smaller submersions and destructions both by wave and volcanic fires. The exultant pulse will beat high in the heart of the race now in the American zone, but there will be no more Americans when the Sixth Race commences; no more, in fact, than Europeans; for they will have now become a *new race, and many new nations*. Yet the Fifth will not die, but survive for a while: overlapping the new Race for many hundred thousands of years to come, it will become transformed with it—slower than its new successor—still getting entirely altered in mentality, general physique, and stature. Mankind will not grow again into giant bodies as in the case of the Lemurians and the Atlanteans; because while the evolution of the Fourth race led the latter down to the very bottom of materiality in its physical development, the present Race is on its ascending arc; and the Sixth will be rapidly growing out of its bonds of matter, and even of flesh.

Thus it is the mankind of the New world—one by far the senior of our Old one, a fact men had also forgotten—of *Pâtâla* (the Antipodes, or the Nether World, as America is called in India), whose mission and Karma it is, to sow the seeds for a forthcoming, grander, and far more glorious Race than any of those we know of at present. The Cycles of Matter will be succeeded by Cycles of Spirituality and a fully developed mind. On the law of parallel history and races, the majority of the future mankind will be composed of glorious Adepts. Humanity is the child of cyclic Destiny, and not one of its Units can escape its unconscious mission, or get rid of the burden of its co-operative work with nature. Thus will mankind, race after race, perform its appointed cycle-pilgrimage. Climates will, and have already begun, to change, each tropical year after the other dropping one sub-race, but only to beget another higher race on the ascending cycle; while a series of other less favoured groups—the failures of nature—will, like some individual men, vanish from the human family without even leaving a trace behind.

Such is the course of Nature under the sway of KARMIC LAW: of the ever present and the ever-becoming Nature. For, in the words of a Sage, known only to a few Occultists:—"THE PRESENT IS THE CHILD OF THE PAST; THE FUTURE, THE BEGOTTEN OF THE PRESENT. AND YET, O PRESENT MOMENT! KNOWEST THOU NOT THAT THOU HAST NO PARENT, NOR CANST THOU HAVE A CHILD; THAT THOU ART EVER BEGETTING BUT THYSELF? BEFORE THOU HAST EVEN BEGUN TO SAY 'I AM THE PROGENY OF THE DEPARTED MOMENT, THE CHILD OF THE PAST,' THOU HAST BECOME THAT PAST ITSELF. BEFORE THOU UTTEREST THE LAST SYLLABLE, BEHOLD! THOU ART NO MORE THE PRESENT BUT VERILY THAT FUTURE. THUS, ARE THE PAST, THE PRESENT, AND THE FUTURE, THE EVER-LIVING TRINITY IN ONE—THE MAHAMAYA OF THE ABSOLUTE IS."

---

claiming the Kumâras "due chiefly to the fancy of the Purànic writers

Ma, ~~we are told by the~~ author of the "Twelve Signs of the Zodiac", is Five; kara, a hand with its

five fingers, as also a five sided sign or a pentagon." The

Kumâra, (in this case an anagram for occult purposes) are

five in esotericism, as Yogis — because the last two names have ~~of days~~ been kept secret; they are the fifth order of Brah-

madevas, and the five fold Chohans, having the soul of the

five [elements] in them, Water and Ether predominating, and

therefore their symbols were both aquatic & fiery. "Wisdom ~~issues from~~ lies concealed under the couch of him who rests on the golden lotos (padma) ~~(lotus)~~ floating on the water." In India it is Vishnu (one of whose avatars was Buddha, as ~~some~~ claimed in days of old). The Prachetasas, the worshippers of Nârâyana (who, like Poseidon moved or dwelt over not under the waters) plunged into the depths of the Ocean for their devotions & remained therein 10,000 years; and the Prachetasas are ten exoterically, but five, esoterically. "Prachetas" is in Sanskrit, the name of ~~the~~ "Varuna, the water god, & the same as Poseidon (Neptune), the Prachetasas being thus identical with the "five ministers" of ΧΩΖΖΑΡ (Poseidon) of the Peratae gnostics, respectively called ΑΟΤ, ΑΟΑΙ, ΟΤΩ, ΟΤΩΑΒ, "the triple name (thus making "seven") of the fifth being lost" — i.e. kept secret. This much for the "aquatic" ... fiery symbol — spiritually. For

Portion of *Secret Doctrine* manuscript page, II:577–8. (TS Archives, Pasadena)

And now to conclude.

We have concerned ourself with the ancient records of the nations, with the doctrine of chronological and psychic cycles, of which these records are the tangible proof; and with many other subjects, which may, at first sight, seem out of place in this volume.

But they were necessary in truth. In dealing with the secret annals and traditions of so many nations, whose very origins have never been ascertained on more secure grounds than inferential suppositions, in giving out the beliefs and philosophy of more than *prehistoric* races, it is not quite as easy to deal with the subject matter as it would be if only the philosophy of one special race, and its evolution, were concerned. The Secret Doctrine is the common property of the countless millions of men born under various climates, in times with which History refuses to deal, and to which esoteric teachings assign dates incompatible with the theories of Geology and Anthropology. The birth and evolution of the Sacred Science of the Past are lost in the very night of Time; and that, even, which is historic — *i.e.*, that which is found scattered hither and thither throughout ancient classical literature—is, in almost every case, attributed by modern criticism to lack of observation in the ancient writers, or to superstition born out of the ignorance of antiquity. It is, therefore, impossible to treat this subject as one would the ordinary evolution of an art or science in some well-known historical nation. It is only by bringing before the reader an abundance of proofs all tending to show that in every age, under every condition of civilization and knowledge, the educated classes of every nation made themselves the more or less faithful echoes of one identical system and its fundamental traditions—that he can be made to see that so many streams of the same water must have had a common source from which they started. What was this source? If coming events are said to cast their shadows before, past events cannot fail to leave their impress behind them. It is, then, by those shadows of the hoary Past and their fantastic silhouettes on the external screen of every religion and philosophy, that we can, by checking them as we go along, and comparing them, trace out finally the body that produced them. There must be truth and fact in that which every people of antiquity accepted and made the foundation of its religions and its faith. Moreover, as Haliburton said, "Hear one side, and you will be in the dark; hear both sides, and all will be clear." The public has hitherto had access to, and heard but one side—or rather the two one-sided views of two diametrically opposed classes of men, whose *primâ facie* propositions or respective premises differ widely, but whose final conclusions are the same—Science and Theology. And now our readers have an opportunity to hear the other—the defendants'—justification and learn the nature of our arguments.

Were the public to be left to its old opinions: namely, on one side, that Occultism, Magic, the legends of old, etc., were all the outcome of ignorance and superstition; and on the other, that everything outside the orthodox groove was the work of the devil, what would be the result? In other words, had no theosophical and mystic literature obtained a hearing for the few last years, the present work would have had a poor chance of impartial consideration. It would have been proclaimed—and by many will still be so proclaimed—a fairy tale woven out of abstruse problems, poised in, and based on the air; built of soap bubbles, bursting at the slightest touch of serious reflection, with *no* foundation, as it would be alleged, to stand upon. Even "the ancient *superstitious* and *credulous* classics" have no word of reference to it in clear and unmistakable terms, and the symbols themselves fail to yield a hint at the existence of such a system. Such would be the verdict of all. But when it becomes undeniably proven that the claim of the modern Asiatic nations to a Secret Science and an esoteric history of the world, is based on fact; that, though hitherto unknown to the masses and a veiled mystery even to the learned, (because they never had the key to a right understanding of the abundant hints thrown out by the ancient classics), it is still no fairy tale, but an actuality—then the present work will become but the pioneer of many more such books. The statement that hitherto even the keys discovered by some great scholars have proved too rusty for use, and that they were but the silent witnesses that there do exist mysteries behind the veil which are unreachable without a new key—is borne out by too many proofs to be easily dismissed. An instance may be given as an illustration out of the history of Freemasonry.

In his "Franc-maçonnerie Occulte," rightly or wrongly, Ragon, an illustrious and learned Belgian Mason, reproaches the English Masons with having *materialized* and dishonoured Masonry, once based upon the Ancient Mysteries, by adopting, owing to a mistaken notion of the origin of the craft, the name of *Free Masonry* and *Free Masons*. The mistake is due, he says, to those who connect Masonry *with the building* of Solomon's Temple, deriving its origin from it. He derides the idea, and says: . . "The *Franc Mason* (which is not *maçon libre*, or free masonry) knew well when adopting the title, that it was no question of *building a wall*, but that of *being initiated into the ancient Mysteries* veiled under the name of *Francmaçonnerie* (Freemasonry); that his work was only to be the continuation or the renovation of the ancient mysteries, and that he was to become a *mason* after the manner of *Apollo* or Amphion. And do not we know that the ancient *initiated* poets, when speaking *of the foundation of a city*, meant thereby the *establishment of a doctrine?* Thus *Neptune*, the god of reasoning, and *Apollo*, the god of the *hidden* things, presented themselves as masons before Laomedon, Priam's father, to help him to build the city of Troy—that is to say, to establish the Trojan religion." (*Maçonnerie Orthodoxe*, p. 44.)

Such *veiled* sentences with double meaning abound in ancient classical writers. Therefore, had an attempt been made to show that, *e.g.*, Laomedon was the founder of a branch of archaic mysteries in which the earth-bound material soul (the fourth principle), was personified in Menelaus' faithless wife (the fair Helen), if Ragon had not come to corroborate what we asserted, we might be told that no classical author speaks of it, and that Homer shows Laomedon building *a city*, not an *esoteric worship* or MYSTERIES! And who are those left now, save a few *Initiates*, who understand the language and correct meaning of such symbolical terms?

But after having pointed to many a misconceived symbol bearing on our thesis, there still remains more than one difficulty to be overcome. Most important among several such obstacles is that of chronology. But this could hardly be helped.

Wedged in between theological chronology and that of the geologists, backed by all the materialistic Anthropologists who assign dates to man and nature which fit in with their own theories alone—what could the writer do except what is being done? Namely, since theology places the Deluge 2448 B.C., and the World's Creation only 5890 years ago; and since the accurate researches by the methods of *exact* Science, have led the geologists and physicists to assign to the incrusted age of our Globe between 10 million and 1,000 million of years* (a *trifling* difference, verily!): and the Anthropologists to vary their divergence of opinion as to the appearance of man—between 25,000 and 500,000 of years—what can one who studies the Occult doctrine do, but come out and bravely present the esoteric calculations before the world?

But to do this, corroboration by even a few "historical" proofs was necessary, though all know the real value of the so-called "historical evidence." For, whether man had appeared on earth 18,000 or 18,000,000 years ago, can make no difference to profane History, since it begins hardly a couple of thousand years before our era, and since, even then, it grapples hopelessly with the clash and din of contradictory and mutually-destroying opinions around it. Nevertheless, in view of the respect the average reader has been brought up in for exact science, even that short *Past* would remain meaningless, unless the esoteric teachings were corroborated and supported on the spot—

---

* *Vide* Sir W. Thomson and Mr. Huxley.

whenever possible—by references to historical names of a so-called *historical* period. This is the only guide that can be given to the beginner before he is permitted to start among the (to him) unfamiliar windings of that dark labyrinth called the pre-historic ages. This necessity has been complied with. It is only hoped that the desire to do so, which has led the writer to be constantly bringing ancient and modern evidence as a corroboration of the Archaic and quite unhistoric Past, will not bring on her the accusation of having sorely jumbled up without order or method the various and widely-separated periods of history and tradition. But literary form and method had to be sacrificed to the greater clearness of the general exposition.

To accomplish the proposed task, the writer had to resort to the rather unusual means of dividing each volume or Book into three Parts; the first of which only is the consecutive, though very fragmentary, history of the Cosmogony and the Evolution of Man on this globe. But these two volumes had to serve as a PROLOGUE, and prepare the reader's mind for those which shall now follow. In treating of Cosmogony and then of the Anthropogenesis of mankind, it was necessary to show that no religion, since the very earliest, has ever been entirely based on fiction, as none was the object of special revelation; and that it is dogma alone which has ever been killing primeval truth. Finally, that no human-born doctrine, no creed, however sanctified by custom and antiquity, can compare in sacredness with the religion of Nature. The Key of Wisdom that unlocks the massive gates leading to the arcana of the innermost sanctuaries can be found hidden in her bosom only: and that bosom is in the countries pointed to by the great seer of the past century Emanuel Swedenborg. There lies the heart of nature, that shrine whence issued the early races of primeval Humanity, and which is the cradle of *physical* man.

Thus far have proceeded the rough outlines of the beliefs and tenets of the archaic, earliest Races contained in their hitherto secret Scriptural records. But our explanations are by no means complete, nor do they pretend to give out the full text, or to have been read by the help of more than three or four keys out of the sevenfold bunch of esoteric interpretation, and even this has only been partially accomplished. The work is too gigantic for any one person to undertake, far more to accomplish. Our main concern was simply to prepare the soil. This, we trust we have done. These two volumes only constitute the work of a pioneer who has forced his way into the well-nigh impenetrable jungle of the virgin forests of the Land of the Occult. A commencement has been made to fell and uproot the deadly upas trees of superstition, prejudice, and conceited ignorance, so that these two volumes should form for the student a fitting prelude for Volumes III. and IV. Until the rubbish of the ages is cleared away from the minds of the Theosophists to whom these volumes are dedicated, it is impossible that the more practical teaching contained in the Third Volume should be understood. Consequently, it entirely depends upon the reception with which Volumes I. and II. will meet at the hands of Theosophists and Mystics, whether these last two volumes will ever be published, though they are *almost* completed.

Satyât Nâsti paro dharmah.

THERE IS NO RELIGION HIGHER THAN TRUTH.

END OF VOL. II.

Overleaf: Galley proof of last page of *The Secret Doctrine* on which HPB inserted in her own handwriting the concluding paragraph. Note minor changes in text in the final printed version. (Original in Archives, TS, Pasadena)

S Seven

To accomplish the proposed task, the writer had to resort to the rather unusual means of dividing each volume or Book into three Parts; the first of which only is the consecutive, though very fragmentary, history of the Cosmogony and the Evolution of Man on this globe. But these two volumes had to serve as a PROLOGUE, and prepare the reader's mind for those which shall now follow. In treating of Cosmogony and now of the Anthropogenesis of mankind, it was necessary to show that no religion, since the very earliest, has ever been entirely based on fiction, as none was the object of special revelation; and that it is dogma which has ever been killing primeval truth. Finally, that no human-born dogma, no institution, however sanctified by custom and antiquity, can compare in sacredness with the dogma of Nature. The Key of Wisdom that unlocks the massive gates leading to the arcana of the innermost sanctuaries can be found hidden in her bosom only; which is in the countries pointed to by the great seer of the past century, Emanuel Swedenborg. There lies the heart of nature, that bosom whence issued the early races of primeval Humanity, and which is the cradle of physical man.

Satyât Nâsti paro dharmah.

THERE IS NO RELIGION HIGHER THAN TRUTH.

END OF VOL. II.

New Para

Thus far have proceeded the rough outlines of the beliefs and tenets of the archaic, earliest Races contained in their hitherto Secret Scriptural records. But our explanations are by [illegible] to give out the full text.

or to have been read by the help of more than three or four keys out of the seven keys of Esoteric interpretation, & even this has been only partially accomplished. The work is too gigantic for any one person to undertake, far more to accomplish. Our main concern was simply to prepare the soil. This, we trust to have done. These two volumes only constitute the work of a pioneer who has forced his way into the well-nigh impenetrable jungle of the virgin forests of the Land of the Occult. A commencement has been made to fell & uproot the deadly Upas trees of Superstition, prejudice & conceited ignorance, so that these two Volumes should form for the student a fitting prelude for Volumes III & IV. Until the rubbish of the ages is cleared away from the minds of the Theosophists to whom these Volumes are dedicated, it is impossible that the more practical teaching contained in the Third Volume should be understood. Consequently, it entirely depends upon the reception with which Volumes I & II will meet at the hands of Theosophists & Mystics, & whether these last two volumes will ever be published, though the Third is ready, & the Fourth almost completed.

The Writing of *The Secret Doctrine*

Kirby Van Mater

THERE CAN BE NO separation between the writings of H. P. Blavatsky and the growth in comprehension of the work of The Theosophical Society by its adherents. As the first teachings of the ancient wisdom — barely sketched in HPB's earliest major work, *Isis Unveiled* — were assimilated, a natural demand was made for a more complete exposition of the philosophy. Likewise the Society's objectives and principles, as enunciated from time to time, became more defined and inclusive of the work envisioned for the Society by those responsible for its beginnings. The true founders of the TS were HPB's teachers, and it was in large measure from them that the subject matter in *Isis Unveiled* and *The Secret Doctrine* was called forth.

Isis Unveiled was commenced in the summer of 1875, a few months before the formation of the TS, although at the time HPB did not know what was to become of the growing pile of manuscripts. Later, in September, as H. S. Olcott records, "She wrote me that it was to be a book on the history and philosophy of the Eastern Schools and their relations with those of our own times."*

In mid-December 1878, a year after the publication of *Isis*, H. P. Blavatsky and Colonel Olcott left New York for India where she carried on her work for the next six years. They soon made the acquaintance of A. P. Sinnett, editor of the Anglo-Indian newspaper, *The Pioneer*. Subsequent correspondence with HPB's teachers — two Eastern Adepts known as M and KH — had a profound effect on him. As a direct result of the inspiration and teaching he had received, and

---

**Old Diary Leaves*, I: 203.

also because of certain phenomena he had personally witnessed, in 1881 Sinnett published *The Occult World* and two years later *Esoteric Buddhism*, two important books which were to produce a considerable stir in various parts of the world. However, in a few instances Sinnett's interpretation of the teachings was incorrect. He also had difficulty in understanding why there were apparent differences in the philosophical *expression* of theosophy as given by his Adept-correspondents and by HPB in *Isis*. He did not comprehend that in *Isis* HPB had been limited as to how much of the ancient wisdom she could give forth. That was in 1877 when the membership had little grasp of the magnitude of theosophy. Within the next five or six years, the time had come to reveal more of the esoteric philosophy and to devise a terminology suitable for Western understanding. KH wrote to Sinnett in 1882:

> It [*Isis*] really ought to be *re-written* for the sake of the family honour. . . . Don't you see that everything you find in *Isis* is delineated, hardly sketched — nothing completed or fully revealed. Well the time has come, but where are the workers for such a tremendous task?
>
> — *The Mahatma Letters to A. P. Sinnett*, letter XXc, 130-1

Nevertheless, starting with the January 1884 issue of the *Journal*,* monthly advertisements appeared describing *The Secret Doctrine* as being a new version of *Isis Unveiled*. That summer in England two students† began writing *Man: Fragments of Forgotten History*. Even before it was published this exposition of theosophical philosophy proved unsatisfactory. On January 9, 1885, HPB was given the "plan" for the great work, *The Secret Doctrine*. Olcott writes:

> On the following night — as my Diary entry states — "H.P.B. got from her Teacher the plan for her *Secret Doctrine*, and it is excellent. Oakley and I tried our hands at it [H.P.B.'s notes and papers on revision of *Isis*] yesterday, but this is much better." Meanwhile, the accumulation of materials for the book had long been going on. It will be news to some that this was not originally intended to be a new book, but only a recasting and amplification of *Isis Unveiled*, with the late T. Subba Row, B.A., B.L., as co-editor with H.P.B. As first advertised in the *Theosophist*, it was to have been issued in monthly parts of 77 pages each, and to have run

---

*Journal of *The Theosophical Society* [Supplement to *The Theosophist*].
†Mohini M. Chatterjee and Laura C. Holloway.

> to about twenty parts. This new scheme, given her by her Teacher, changed this programme, and the gradual building up of the present grand work was the result.*
> — *ODL*, III: 199-200

The previous year, in February 1884, HPB, Olcott, and four companions had left Bombay for Europe. While they were away a carefully planned attack was begun against HPB and indirectly the Theosophical Society by Alexis and Emma Coulomb (who had been taken into the headquarters at Adyar) and the editors of the *Christian College Magazine* in Madras. HPB was charged with forgery in producing letters from her teachers as well as trickery in the production of phenomena. The effect of this attack was immediate worldwide publicity and the return to India of both Olcott and Blavatsky by year's end. At this time the Society for Psychical Research sent to India a young man named Richard Hodgson to investigate and report on the situation.

In their efforts not to cause more publicity and expose the names of the Mahatmas to public eye, Olcott and the TS Council at Adyar left HPB undefended, and thus by their silence virtually implied her guilt. HPB strenuously objected; the honor of the Society and of her teachers was at stake. She had wished to go to court in order to vindicate her teachers and the work they had sent her to do. But Olcott threatened HPB with his resignation if she did not abide by the decision of the Special Judicial Committee.† Eventually her already poor health broke down. On March 21 HPB tendered her resignation as Corresponding Secretary, and on the 31st on doctor's orders she left India, hopefully to recover sufficiently to finish her *Secret Doctrine*. As she was boarding the steamer, Subba Row asked HPB to continue writing and send him through Olcott every week what she had written, as he would then "make notes and commentaries" (*The Theosophist*, March 1925, 784).

Even on the open sea, she received "pages of manuscript referring to *The Secret Doctrine*."‡ She stayed about three months in Italy, at Torre del Greco and Rome, and later in Switzerland, finally settling at

---

*One purpose of *The Secret Doctrine* was to correct errors in philosophy in *Esoteric Buddhism* and *Man: Fragments of Forgotten History.*

†Annual Convention TS, Dec. 1884; cf. *Lucifer*, Aug. 15, 1891 (VIII: 447).

‡Cf. Constance Wachtmeister, *Reminiscences of H. P. Blavatsky and "The Secret Doctrine,"* letter of F. Hartmann to Mrs. Vera Johnston, June 2nd, 1893, 109.

Würzburg, Germany in early August. On October 28, 1885, HPB wrote Olcott that she had "not much time now . . . but shall in a month or two send you the first six sections." (*ODL*, III: 317).

But no real work was done until December when Countess Wachtmeister came to be a companion and helper to HPB. Saved now from continual interruptions which had plagued her previously, HPB was able to keep a schedule of writing day after day through the long hours. In the months that followed only three times was the Countess able to prevail upon her to leave the apartment.

But December was hardly over when HPB received the *Proceedings* of the Society for Psychical Research based on Hodgson's investigations in India. This account was as unfair to her as was the earlier attack by the Coulombs and the *Christian College Magazine*.* It is difficult to imagine the impact of this report upon HPB. Countess Wachtmeister relates:

> "This," she cried, "is the Karma of the Theosophical Society, and it falls upon me. I am the scapegoat. I am made to bear all the sins of the Society, and now that I am dubbed the greatest impostor of the age, and a Russian spy into the bargain, who will listen to me or read *The Secret Doctrine?*"
> — Wachtmeister, *Reminiscences*, 26

On January 6, 1886, HPB wrote to Olcott that *The Secret Doctrine* would be the vindication of herself and her teachers.

> For Secret Doctrine *is entirely* new. There will not be there 20 pages quoted by bits from *Isis*. . . . In *four* Parts — Archaic, Ancient, Mediaeval and Modern Periods. Each Part 12 chapters, with Appendices and a Glossary of terms at the end. Countess here, and she sees I have almost *no books*. Master and Kashmiri† dictating in turn. She copies all.
> — *Theos.*, Aug. 1931, 667

---

*The April 1986 *Journal of the Society for Psychical Research* printed an article entitled "J'ACCUSE: An Examination of the Hodgson Report of 1885" by Vernon Harrison, a senior member of the SPR and an acknowledged expert on handwriting and forgery. Dr. Harrison's critique concludes (p. 309):

> "[Richard Hodgson's] report is riddled with slanted statements, conjecture advanced as fact or probable fact, uncorroborated testimony of unnamed witnesses, selection of evidence and downright falsity. . . . His case against Madame H. P. Blavatsky is not proven."

†M and KH.

HPB stayed at Würzburg from August 1885 till May 1886. About the end of April she decided to spend the summer months at Ostende, Belgium, with her sister and niece. However, en route Gustav and Mary Gebhard persuaded her to visit their home at Elberfeld, Germany, and while there HPB injured her leg. It was not until July that she settled in Ostende where the Countess soon joined her, and once again the writing for the *SD* continued without interruption.

In the evening after her day's work, HPB was not averse to reading to visitors what she had written if she felt they would be interested. She also gave sections of the manuscript to different individuals to read. Eight pages were sent to Sinnett to share with Sir William Crookes, the most eminent chemist of his day in England and also a theosophist. On a number of occasions manuscripts were mailed to Adyar both from Würzburg and Ostende. At one time HPB sent a large section to Olcott, warning him and Subba Row not to lose it.

> Do, however, as you please, . . . and if you want to add write the addition on page and pin it to the page you add to. Remember, this is my last *great work*. I could not rewrite it if lost to save my life or that of the Society which is more. — *Theos.*, March 1925, 790

In *Old Diary Leaves* (III: 385), Olcott writes that the *SD* manuscript of Volume I arrived in December 1886, but that Subba Row would not work on it as originally agreed upon because, as he said, there were so many errors he would have to rewrite it. HPB, much distressed, carefully went over the material again making many corrections.

Earlier, on October 21, she had written Olcott that in the spring she would go to London because of the availability of books at the Museum for checking, and also she would have proofreaders among the members there. Later, when Subba Row flatly refused to look at the material, HPB asks what should she do now without his help for the second volume, "where I have any number of Sanskrit words and sentences, and the esoteric meaning of any number of exoteric Hindu allegories from their Cosmogony and Theogony . . ."

> Please answer immediately. The whole almost is given by the "old gentleman" and Master and there *are* wonderful things there I tell you. But someone must see to the Sanskrit and the corrections of the *exoteric* renderings. — Ibid., 787

In England at this time, a number of members of Sinnett's London Lodge were not satisfied with the existing state of affairs. They felt that a new impulse was needed for public work,* and they decided to write HPB individually about the problem. Each received a long letter in return in which, among other things, she explained the urgency for her to finish *The Secret Doctrine* before taking up other activities. Nevertheless, early in 1887 Bertram Keightley went to Ostende to see HPB, who asked him "to look over parts of the MSS." She agreed to come to London at the end of April, provided lodging and other matters could be arranged. Soon after, Dr. Archibald Keightley† went to Ostende to visit HPB, who likewise gave him some of the *SD* to read. But hardly had he returned to England when news came of HPB's grave illness. Her physician and friends thought this time she would surely die but, as she had done in India in February 1885, she again miraculously recovered. Almost immediately thereafter she announced that the next phase of her work was to be carried on in England, both as regards *The Secret Doctrine* and the Theosophical Society. Learning of this, the Keightleys went to Ostende in the last weeks of April to prepare for the move. She was to stay at the small home of Mrs. Mabel Cook (Mabel Collins), Maycot, Upper Norwood, London.

HPB describes her move in a card to William Q. Judge:‡

> Maycot, Crownhill. Upper Norwood. London C.S. May 7th.
>
> "Oh *thy* prophetic Soul!" Didn't know old HPB was for 17 days hovering between life & death; drawn irresistibly by the charm *beyond* the latter & held by her coat-tails by the Countess & some London Lodges? Nice intuitional friend. Anyhow, *saved* once more, & once more stuck into the mud of life right with my classical nose. Two Keightleys & Thornton (a dear, *real* new Theosophist) came to Ostende, packed me up, books, kidneys & gouty legs & carried me across the water partially in steamer, partially in invalid chair & the rest in train to Norwood in one of the cottages of which here I am, living (rather *vegetating*) in it till the Countess returns. Write here "1000 words for the Path"? I'll TRY, old man. Very, very seedy & weak; but rather better after the mortal disease

---

*Bertram Keightley, *Reminiscences of H.P.B.*, 1931, and Archibald Keightley, "From Ostende To London," *The Path*, November 1892, 245.

†Uncle of Bertram, although one year younger.

‡Archives, Theosophical Society, Pasadena.

HPB at "Maycot," Upper Norwood, London, 1887

which *cleansed* me if it did not carry me off. Love & sincere, as usual, & for ever. Yours in heaven & hell. "O.L." HPB.

As soon as possible she was at her desk and work went on as usual. The task of readying the *SD* for publication fell mainly to the Keightleys. Bertram Keightley wrote that on arriving in England HPB asked them what they wished to do and after hearing their replies remarked, "All right, then, . . . here you are — get to work right away" (BK, *Reminiscences*, 7). With that she gave them the entire manuscript to go through and advise her about arranging it. It made a pile over three feet high and was, as Archibald Keightley relates, "in detached sections, . . . with no definite arrangement, much of which had been patiently and industriously copied by the Countess Wachtmeister." After prolonged consultations the plan submitted to HPB became the present division of the volumes and contents. Other material having no place in the order and plan was to be saved for the future. They worked through the summer "reading, re-reading, copying, and correcting."* There were many quotations to be verified at the British Museum or wherever else they might be located.

It should be mentioned that the Stanzas of Dzyan, on which *The Secret Doctrine* is based, had little commentary in the first drafts of the book. To HPB they were perfectly understandable, but for the student explanations were needed. A plan was arrived at whereby a Stanza was written out on a blank sheet of paper, and questions pinned to it, to which HPB would write answers. Often she demanded clarifications of the questions before attempting her comments. Yet with all this work on the *SD* going on, HPB founded a new magazine, *Lucifer*, the first issue of which appeared in September 1887. That same month she moved to larger quarters at 17 Lansdowne Road. The spirit and enthusiasm of those working with her show up clearly in the following extract from a letter dated May 28, 1887, from Bertram Keightley to W. Q. Judge:†

H.P.B is fairly well & working away right hard at the Secret Doctrine; which is *awfully good* & I am sure you will be immensely pleased with it. Tho' I date this from Linden Gardens, I am staying with HPB at Maycot, Crown Hill, Upper Norwood. S.E where I expect she will be for the next two or three months. We have got a scheme on foot for establishing

---

*Wachtmeister, *Reminiscences*, 97, 91, 98. †Archives, TS, Pasadena.

> HPB in *winter* quarters near London where she can live in peace & gather the real workers in the Society around her. But whether it will succeed or even ever be really begun I cannot tell. All I know is that we shall do our level best to bring it about. Still do *not mention* anything about it; as "there's many a slip twixt the cup & the lip" & these things are best kept quiet till actually done. Anyway we mean a real effort to put new life into this dull L.L. [London Lodge] & the new Magazine, is the first step. The title at present in favour is "*Lucifer: the Lightbearer*," but no final decision has yet been come to. At any rate we *mean to do two things*: to make HPB as comfortable as we can & to prove to her that there are some at least who really appreciate her ceaseless self sacrifice & untiring exertions for the Cause.

After much cutting, pasting, and typing of clear copies of most of Volumes I and II, the manuscript finally was sent to press. Then came the task of proofreading, and this too had its challenges, as Archibald Keightley recalled:

> The *Secret Doctrine* began to be printed and in this and in Lucifer Mme. Blavatsky's idiosyncrasy of regarding page-proof as being equivalent to manuscript, led to much argument and expense. It was not merely that she would divide a page after the type was all locked in the forms and insert a quantity of fresh matter, but she would with much care and precision of scissors cut out and then paste in a single sentence in an entirely different place. Woe betide the zealous sub-editor who protested on behalf of the printers and the provision of funds. "Off with his head" or his metaphysical scalp were the orders of the Queen of our wonderland. Nevertheless the account for corrections of the *Secret Doctrine* came to more than the original cost of setting up!
>
> — "Reminiscences of H. P. Blavatsky," *Theosophical Quarterly* (VIII: 30), 115

HPB had long been disappointed with her financial arrangements with J. W. Bouton of New York for the publication of *Isis Unveiled* and, in consequence, she was determined to have financial control of *The Secret Doctrine* in both the United States and England. In May 1888 she asked W. Q. Judge to secure copyright in her name in the United States for her book, and to publish it in the U.S. either from "stereo plates, or only the moulds" sent from England.* Judge, after consul-

*Letter, Bertram Keightley to W. Q. Judge, May 29, 1888, countersigned by HPB (Archives, TS, Pasadena).

tation with J. W. Lovell (of John W. Lovell Co. of New York), wrote Bert Keightley that the best method to follow for 1,000 sheets or more was for London to ship printed sheets, to be folded, collated, and bound in the U.S.* Copyright could be obtained in HPB's name as she was an American citizen, if all particulars about the book were furnished as requested. However, HPB was to understand "that the emission of the American and English editions should be simultaneous."† After delays in England the sheets, folded and collated, for 1,000 copies of the first volume of the *SD* arrived in New York City on the steamer *Britannia*, Friday, October 19th. Judge wrote that the deadline of October 27th for "publishing" probably could not be met by him.‡ Finally, on October 31st H. P. Blavatsky cabled Judge asking "Have you published?" Judge cabled back "Yes, Book Out Nov 1."§ Volume II was published December 28th.

Questions as to who wrote *The Secret Doctrine* and how it was written have been asked ever since the book appeared. HPB made no claim for the entire production. As she explained to Sinnett in her letter of March 3, 1886:

> There's a new development and scenery, every morning. I *live two lives again*. Master finds that it is too difficult for me to be looking consciously into the astral light for my S.D. and so, it is now about a fortnight, I am made to see all I have to as though in my dream. I see large and long rolls of paper on which things are written and I recollect them. — *The Letters of H. P. Blavatsky to A. P. Sinnett*, 194

The Master KH gives further insight into the writing of the *SD* in his letter to Olcott, August 1888:

> I have also noted, your thoughts about the "Secret Doctrine". Be assured that what she has not *annotated* from scientific and other works, we have given or *suggested* to her. Every mistake or erroneous notion, corrected and explained by her from the works of other theosophists *was corrected by me, or under my instruction*. It is a more valuable work than its

---

*Letter, J. W. Lovell to W. Q. Judge, June 12, 1888, and Letter, WQJ to BK, June 22, 1888 (Archives, TS, Pasadena).

†Letter, WQJ to BK, June 22, 1888 (Archives, TS, Pasadena).

‡Letter, WQJ to BK, October 19, 1888 (Archives, TS, Pasadena).

§Archives, TS, Pasadena.

predecessor [*Isis*], an epitome of occult truths that will make it a source of information and instruction for the earnest student for long years to come. — *Letters from the Masters of the Wisdom*, No. 19, I:47, 5th ed.

The co-authorship of *The Secret Doctrine* is also made plain in joint letters from the Mahatmas M and KH to Dr. Hübbe-Schleiden, received by him in Germany in early January 1886. Copies of these letters in Masters' handwriting were sent by HPB to Judge in America for his future use. He printed them with explanations in the April 1893 issue of *The Path*. The letters are reproduced on the following pages.

Any work, of course, must stand on its merit rather than on the means by which it was produced. Every reader must judge for himself how well HPB carried out her purposes. As she states in her Preface, *The Secret Doctrine* was "written in the service of humanity, and by humanity and the future generations it must be judged."

As the last sentences of Volume II indicate, HPB had two further volumes in preparation to be issued if the reception of the first volumes warranted it. These were never published and one can only surmise that more time was needed to comprehend the material already given out. She did, however, produce *The Voice of the Silence*, a small book of precepts drawn from "the same series as that from which the 'Stanzas' of the *Book of Dzyan* were taken, on which the *Secret Doctrine* is based." These present a noble conduct of life for those who would make themselves of greater service to mankind, and it was hoped that perhaps some few might find access to that inner knowledge to which she had pointed the way. As to Volumes III and IV, who is to say they will ever be issued.

Today, a century after the publication of *The Secret Doctrine*, other egos are creating a new world. The teachings they call forth for the next century will be in answer to their karma and the karma of their times. If HPB's writings have produced any effect, it may be found in the deeper spiritual yearning among an ever greater number to bring about the Universal Brotherhood for which she so labored and sacrificed.

The following letters regarding the "triple" authorship of *The Secret Doctrine* were written by the Mahatmas M and KH. These facsimile reproductions are made from originals in the Archives of the Theosophical Society, Pasadena.

LETTER ONE is a copy made by the Mahatmas of their original messages to Dr. Hübbe-Schleiden of Germany. Upasika stands for HPB.

Side One, written in blue crayon by KH, reads:

> To Hubbe Schleiden — copy.
>
> I wonder if this note of mine is worthy of occupying a select spot with the documents reproduced and which of the peculiarities of the "Blavatskian" style of writing it will be found to most resemble? The present is simply to satisfy the D^r "the more proof given the less believed." Let him take my advice and not make these two documents public. It is for his own satisfaction the undersigned is happy to assure him that the Secret Doctrine when ready, will be the triple production of M∴ Upasika and the Doctors most humble servant.
>
> K.H.
>
> S.E.C.

Side Two, written diagonally in red crayon by M and now very faint, reads:

> If this can be of any use or help to Dr. Hubbe Schleiden — though I doubt it — I the humble undersigned Fakir certify that the Secret Doctrine is dictated to Upasika partly by myself and partly by my Brother K.H.
>
> M∴

To Hubbe Schleiden – copy.

I wonder if this note of mine is worthy of occupying a select spot with the documents reproduced and which of the peculiarities of the "Blavatskian" style of writing it will be found to most resemble? The present is simply to satisfy the Dr. "the more proof given the less believed." Let him take my advice and not make these two documents public. It is for his own satisfaction the undersigned is happy to assure him that the Secret Doctrine when ready, will be the triple production of M∴ Upasika and the Doctor's most humble servant K.H.

S.E.C.

The certificate given last year saying that the Secret Doctrine would be when finished the triple production of Upasika M. and myself was and is correct, although some have doubted not only the facts given in it but also the authenticity of the message in which it was contained. Copy this and also keep the copy of the aforesaid certificate. You will find them both of use on the day when you shall, as will happen without your asking, receive from the hands of the very person to whom the certificate was given, the original for the purpose of allowing you to copy it; and then you can verify the correctness of this presently forwarded copy. And it may then be well to indicate to those wishing to know what portions in the Secret Doctrine have been copied by the pen of Upasika into its pages, though without quotation marks, from my own manuscript and perhaps from me though the last is more difficult from the rarity of his know writing and greater ignorance of his style. All this and more will be found necessary as time goes on but for which you are well qualified to wait.

K. H.

The [illegible] will be in the same [illegible] C.B. [illegible] besides [illegible] least perfect it [illegible] is not in the letters [illegible] style — the [illegible] D — [illegible] the whole [illegible]

Letter Two, sent the following year by M and KH, repeats the original statement concerning the authorship of *The Secret Doctrine*. The portion written by KH is in blue crayon, the second half of the reverse side being written diagonally in red crayon by M. The texts read:

The certificate given last year saying that the Secret Doctrine would be when finished the triple production of Upasika M.˙. and myself was and is correct, although some have doubted not only the facts given in it but also the authenticity of the message in which it was contained. Copy this and also keep the copy of the aforesaid certificate. You will find them both of use on the day when you shall, as will happen without your asking, receive from the hands of the very person to whom the certificate was given, the original for the purpose of allowing you to copy it;[*] and then you can verify the correctness of this presently forwarded copy. And it may then be well to indicate to those wishing to know what portions in the Secret Doctrine have been copied by the pen of Upasika into its pages, though without quotation marks, from my own manuscript and perhaps from M.˙. though the last is more difficult from the rarity of his know(n) writing and greater ignorance of his style. All this and more will be found necessary as time goes on but for which you are well qualified to wait.

K.H.

The Dr. will be in the same rut for many years. Go on and fear nothing. I am beside you when you least expect it. No, this is not my personal style — the latter in a language you could not read — Yes right, the whole age transits — Particulars not given

M.˙.

---

*[In his Diary, under date of July 21 (1892), London, William Q. Judge writes: ". . . Hubbe Schleiden arrives had conference. . . . He lends me masters letters to him. Same as copies sent me by H.P.B." — KVM]

Glossary

Adam Kadmon — (Heb) In the Kabbalah, archetypal or primordial humanity, macrocosmic or Heavenly Man in contradistinction to the earthly Adam; the Sephirothal Tree of Life.

Ādi-Sanat — (Skt) "First Ancient," title of Brahmā, highest manifesting divinity.

Ah-hi — (Senzar) Dhyāni-chohans, primordial seven logoi, the elohīm, a class of celestial beings through which universal mind manifests.

Akasha, Ākāśa — (Skt, fr *kāś*, "to shine") "space, vacuity," aether, the fifth cosmic element; subtle spiritual essence or substance which pervades all space.

Alaya — (Skt) The "indissoluble"; in Buddhism the universal soul or mahābuddhi.

Amānasa — (Skt) The mindless, protohuman races.

Amshaspend(s) — (Pahlavi) In Zoroastrianism, "immortal benefactors," the six or seven creative deities, aspects of Ahura Mazda; similar to the elohīm or sephīrōth.

Anupapādaka — (Skt) "Parentless," self-born or -existing; applied in Buddhism to certain self-created gods and dhyāni-buddhas.

Arhat — (Skt) High initiate; in Buddhism, those who have attained nirvana; more generally, an ascetic.

Arūpa — (Skt) "Formless," unmanifest.

Aryan Race — (Skt, fr *ārya*, "noble") Indo-European people who migrated into Northern India, Āryāvarta; in theosophy applied to the 5th root-race (present humanity).

Asura(s) — (Skt) A "not-god" in post-Vedic period, demons or evil spirits hostile to the *suras* (gods); in the most ancient portions of the *Ṛig Veda*, divine beings, supreme spirit (possibly fr *asu*, "breath"); in theosophy, intellectual deities.

Ātman — (Skt) "Self," universal spirit, the highest consciousness in all entities, including man.

Bhāshya — (Skt) A treatise or commentary.

Bhūta — (Skt) A "has-been"; ghost or astral shell of a deceased person minus soul and spirit.

Brahma(n) — (Skt) The impersonal, absolute, ultimate reality; the unmanifest Logos.

Brahmā — (Skt) Hindu creator god; individualized, periodical generative aspect of Brahman; hierarch of a universe.

Buddhi — (Skt, fr *budh*, "to wake up") Human spiritual soul, principle of intuitive knowledge.

Chhāyā — (Skt) A "shade, shadow," the astral or model body.

Chhāyā-loka — (Skt) Shadow of cosmic spirit; also the sphere of shades, kāma-loka.

Chohan(s) — "Lord," superior chief, divine or human.

Crore — Ten million.

Ḍākiṇī — (Skt) Female demons attendant on Kālī; mindless elemental beings in female form; equivalent to Khado.

Dangma — (Tib) Freed or purified soul, a high adept, mahatma.

De minimus non curat lex — (Lat) The law does not concern itself with trifles.

Demiourgos — (Gk) Cosmic artificer, supreme architect; collectively, the creative powers which build the universe.

Devamātṛi — (Skt) "Mother of the gods," cosmic or mystic space.

Dhyāni(s) — (Skt, fr *dhyāna*, "deep contemplation") Spiritual beings.

Dhyāni-Buddha — (Skt) A spiritual architect of worlds who emanates divine creative forces, the cosmic prototype of a human buddha.

Dhyāni-Chohan(s) — "Lords of meditation," creative gods, celestial beings superior to man.

Dzyan — A "corruption" of Skt *dhyāna* (spiritual "meditation") and *jñāna* (wisdom, divine knowledge).

Dzyu — Real knowledge; the collective wisdom of the dhyāni-buddhas which becomes fohat.

Elementals — Ethereal beings born from and animating the elements; classes of beings evolutionally lower than the minerals.

Elohīm — (Heb, plural) Gods, usually translated God; corresponds to the creative logoi or hosts emanated from the First Logos.

Facies totius Universi . . . (Spinoza) — "The face of the whole universe, though it varies in infinite modes, yet remains always the same."

Fohat — (Turanian compound, fr Mongolian *pho*, *fo*, "buddha, buddhi") The cause or essence of cosmic vitality or electricity, divine ideative energy of the universe.

Fons et origo — (Lat) Source and origin.

Jīva — (Skt) Individualized "life" force, a living being or monad; also cosmic life principle, prāna.

Jñāna Yoga — (Skt) "Union" with the divine through "knowledge" and wisdom.

Kabbalah — (Heb) The esoteric "tradition" or theosophy of the Jews.

Kabiri — (Gk, *kabeiroi*, possibly of Phrygian origin) Divine instructors of arts, sciences, and agriculture, linked with cosmic and terrestrial fire; also, regents of seasons and cosmic cycles.

Kalpa — (Skt) An age or vast time cycle.

Kāma — (Skt) "Desire"; love in all its ranges, cosmic and human.

Kāraṇa — (Skt) "Cause" of existence and of death, the Causeless Cause.

Karma — (Skt) "Action" and reaction, cause and effect, absolute justice and harmony.

Khado or Khadomas — (Tib) Female demons, mindless elemental beings in female form, equivalent of Skt *ḍākiṇī*.

Kriyāśakti — (Skt) "Power of action," the creative power of thought and spiritual will.

Kshatriya — (Skt) In Hinduism, a member of the warrior, administrator, and ruler class.

Kwan-Shi-Yin — (Chin) Male aspect of divine wisdom, the first manifested Logos or the seventh (highest) universal principle.

Kwan-Yin — (Chin) Buddhist "goddess of compassion," female aspect of Kwan-Shi-Yin.

Kwan-Yin-Tien — (Chin) "Melodious heaven of sound," abode of Kwan-Yin.

Lanoo — Student, disciple, chela.

Lha(s) — (Tib) Celestial beings ranging from the highest to a terrestrial spirit; equivalent to Skt *deva*.

Lhamayin — (Tib) Non-deity, demon, elemental; spirits of lower spheres; equivalent to Skt *asura*.

Life-wave — Kingdom or family of monads which progress through the 7 globes of a planetary chain.

Lipika — (Skt) "Scribe," celestial recorders on the astral light of every thought, word, and act; highest cosmic agents of karma.

Logos — (Gk) "Word," manifested deity, the living expression of divine thought.

Lusus naturae — (Lat) Freak of nature.

Mahābuddhi — (Skt) "Great buddhi," cosmic intelligence or mind, source of human mind.

Mahat — (Skt) The "great"; cosmic mind or intelligence; source of manas.

Manas — (Skt, fr *man*, "to think") Self-conscious mind, human intelligence.

Mānasa — (Skt) Adjectival form of manas: *mānasa-dhyāni*, *mānasaputras*, mind-born sons of Brahmā.

Māṇḍūkya — (Skt) An Upanishad dealing with the sacred syllable Om.

Manu — (Skt) Progenitor of mankind; collectively, the pitṛis or entities who begin and end a planetary life cycle.

Mānushya — (Skt) "Human," especially a human buddha who guides and inspires a root-race or life-wave.

Manvantara — (Skt) "Between manus," a period of manifested life which alternates with rest periods (pralayas).

Mātṛipadma — (Skt) Mother lotus.

Māyā, Mahāmāyā — (Skt) "Illusion," the noneternal, that causes us not to perceive reality as it is.

Metempsychosis — (Gk) "Reensoulment," the progress of a monad through soul after soul; an aspect of reimbodiment.

Mlechchhas — (Skt) "Outcastes"; in Hinduism, foreigners, barbarians; also those unworthy of esoteric learning.

Monad(s) — (fr Gk *monas*, "one, unit") Indivisible, divine center of every living being, atomic to cosmic.

Mūlaprakṛiti — (Skt) "Root-nature," undifferentiated cosmic substance, the veil or opposite pole of Parabrahman.

Mutatis mutandis — (Lat) Necessary changes being made.

Nāstika — (Skt) "Atheist," unbeliever, one who does not worship idols or the anthropomorphic gods of orthodox religions.

Nidānas — (Skt) "Bonds," in Buddhism, the twelve causes of existence, the chain of causation.

Nirvāṇa — (Skt) "Blown out," liberation from material existence; absolute consciousness.

Occult(ist) — (fr Lat *occultus*, "hid") Concealed, obscured by something else, as in astronomy; a truth seeker, adept in hidden wisdom and knowledge.

Oeaohoo — The "7-voweled" sacred name representing the sevenfold root from which all proceeds; parent of the gods.

Parabrahm(an) — (Skt) "Beyond Brahman," precosmic source of divinity and being, the Ineffable, unnameable That; also spiritual pole of mūlaprakṛiti.

Paramārtha — (Skt) True or supreme self-consciousness; in Buddhism, absolute or nirvanic consciousness.

Paranishpanna, paranirvāṇa or parinirvāṇa — (Skt) "Beyond nirvana"; the state when all life is withdrawn into the divine source and all matter is dissolved (cosmic pralaya).

Pitṛi(s) — (Skt) "Fathers," progenitors of the human race.

Prakṛiti — (Skt) Primal nature, spiritual and etheral substance; opposite pole of Purusha.

Pralaya — (Skt) "Dissolution," death, a period of latency between manvantaras, planetary or cosmic.

Pro re natā — (Lat) For a special emergency or business.

Purāṇa(s) — (Skt) "Ancient" stories; collections of Hindu allegories and myths on cosmic and human life-cycles.

Purusha — (Skt) "Ideal or cosmic man," Hindu equivalent of Adam Kadmon; the universal spirit that animates prakṛiti, its substantial counterpart or pole; the individual spiritual self or monad of any entity.

Root-Race(s) — The main serial divisions of the life-waves on any planetary globe, each lasting millions of years; present-day humanity comprises the 5th of 7 great root-races.

Round(s) — The procession of any life-wave through all the globes of a planetary chain; also the completion of 7 root-races on any one globe (globe-round).

Rūpa — (Skt) Form, body.

Sapta — (Skt) Seven.

Saptasarma [Saptaparṇa] — (Skt) "Seven-leaved parṇa tree," the man-plant, the seven-principled human being.

Sat — (Skt) "Truth, reality, pure being" — the essence of Brahman.

Senzar — Mystic name for the secret sacerdotal language, the "Mystery-speech" of initiated adepts; original language of the Stanzas of Dzyan.

Sephīrōth — (Heb) In the Kabbalah, the ten divine emanations from *Ain Soph* (the Boundless) which form the Tree of Life or tenfold universe.

Sien-Tchan — (Chin) The material universe, world of illusion.

Silent Watcher — The summit of a hierarchy; the terrestrial Silent Watcher is the Mahāguru, the Great Sacrifice, who renounces nirvana and individual progress for the sake of all lower sentient beings.

Śishṭa(s) — (Skt) "Residue, remainders," those left behind; the most evolved representatives of each kingdom which remain behind at the end of a cycle to serve as seeds for that kingdom in the next cycle.

Śloka — (Skt) Verse of a stanza; the usual Sanskrit epic meter of 32 syllables.

Soma — (Skt) Hindu male lunar deity; also a "beverage" from a sacred plant which can induce spiritual vision.

Stanzas of Dzyan — Source text of *The Secret Doctrine*, excerpted from Chinese, Tibetan, and Sanskrit translations of the original Senzar commentaries and glosses on the *Book of Dzyan*.

Sūtrātma — (Skt) "Thread-self," the abiding self or soul which survives death, the spiritual essence (ātman), stream of self-consciousness, individuality, or thread of radiance upon which the personalities of its various incarnations are strung.

Svabhavat — (Skt) "Self-existent," cosmic consciousness-substance, the reservoir of Being, ākāśa.

Tridaśa — (Skt) "Thrice ten," in round numbers the sum of the Hindu pantheon, 330 million deities (lives).

Upādhi — (Skt) "Vehicle" or body on any plane.

Upanishad — (Skt) Esoteric doctrine; philosophical texts belonging to the Vedic cycle.

Vāhana — (Skt) "Vehicle" or form imbodying a consciousness.

Veda(s) — (Skt) "Knowledge," oldest, most sacred collection of Hindu scriptures: *Ṛig-veda*, *Sāma-veda*, *Yajur-veda*, and *Atharva-veda*, each containing 4 divisions of text — Saṃhitā, Brāhmaṇa, Āraṇyaka, and Upanishad.

Vedānta — (Skt) "End or completion of the Vedas"; one of the six main Brahmanical schools.

Vidyā — (Skt) "Wisdom, knowledge," esoteric science.

Völuspá — "The Sibyl's Prophecy," mystic poem opening the Elder Edda, the Norse theosophy.

Yati — A measure of length, about 3 feet.